Bought

THE SACRED KNOWLEDGE

Altaf al-Quds

THE SACRED KNOWLEDGE
OF THE
HIGHER FUNCTIONS OF THE MIND

Altaf al-Quds

by
Shah Waliullah of Delhi

Translated by
Professor G. N. Jalbani

Revised and Edited by
David Pendlebury

THE OCTAGON PRESS
LONDON

Copyright © 1982 by The Octagon Press Limited.
All Rights Reserved.
No part of this publication may be reproduced or transmitted
in any form or by any means, electronic, mechanical or
photographic, by recording or any information storage or retrieval
system or method now known or to be invented or adapted,
without prior permission obtained in writing from the publisher,
The Octagon Press Limited
14, Baker Street, London W1M 1DA, England
except by a reviewer quoting brief passages in a
review written for inclusion in a
journal, magazine, newspaper or broadcast.

ISBN: 90086093 6

Photoset, printed and bound in Great Britain by
Redwood Burn Limited, Trowbridge, Wiltshire

CONTENTS

		Page
Preface by the Translator		vi
Introduction by Shah Waliullah		1
1	The Knowledge of the Higher Functions	3
2	The Nature of the Soul	7
3	The Manifest Faculties	16
4	Holy Law and the Manifest Faculties	23
5	The Teaching of Junaid	36
6	The Hidden Faculties	64
7	Thoughts and their Causes	95

PREFACE BY THE TRANSLATOR

Ahmad b. Abdurrahim al Umari, popularly known as Shah Waliullah, was born near Delhi in 1702 and died in 1762. He was not only a great theologian but also a Sufi of the highest rank. The services which he and his descendants rendered to humanity were abundant and far-reaching in their consequences. In the field of mysticism his contemporaries were, generally speaking, inadequately educated and influenced to a considerable degree by non-Islamic elements. This had given rise to a variety of innovations and superstitions.

Shah Waliullah presented religion in its authentic form—as it had existed during the first two centuries of the Islamic era—and removed all the worthless and disfiguring accretions of subsequent periods. He is known to have written about fifty books.

This present work, *Altaf-al-Quds fi Ma'arifat Lataif-in-Nafs*, occupies a very high position in Sufi literature. It is concerned with the inner dimensions of mysticism, and presents a detailed discussion of the hidden faculties of humanity, shedding ample light on the questions of ecstatic intuition and mystical revelation.

It has long been a habit of mystics to mix one reality with another and refer to both by the same name. This has frequently given rise to confusion as to what they really meant. For example, when they use the word *nafs* (self), sometimes they mean the source of life, i.e., the soul, while at other times they mean human nature. Similarly, when they use the word *qalb* (heart) they are sometimes referring to the conical piece of flesh and sometimes to the faculty of perception. Likewise, when they mention the word *ruh* (soul), they sometimes mean the source of life, and sometimes a pure and subtle substance pervading the entire body; occasionally even they mean the angelic soul, which was created long before the actual creation of mankind. In the same way they have often confused the objective meaning of a word with the subjective associations which that word may acquire, and have failed to make a distinction between the two.

Shah Waliullah says that every mystic has interpreted reality in accordance with his capacity, and that it is precisely this basic difference in capacity which has caused the differences in their interpretations. Furthermore, the variations in technical terms used by them have led their readers to confuse what are in fact separate realities. As Shah Waliullah explicitly stated, he had arrived at the ultimate mystical goal; hence he was able clearly to distinguish one reality from another, place each word in its proper place, and remove ambiguity wherever he found it.

G. N. Jalbani
Hyderabad, May 1979.

INTRODUCTION

To God be all praise, for showing his sincere servants the signs of his greatness both in the universe at large and within their own selves, until at last it becomes clear to them that he alone is real. All things material and spiritual existing in the universe are in his charge; and he subsists by virtue of his essence and his attributes. All but God is false. He encompasses the whole of existence in every direction and in all its aspects. Wherever you turn your face, there is the face of God. I bear witness that there is no god but God, and that Muhammad is his servant and messenger. May God shower his blessings upon him—upon his family and his companions!

And now, that needy suppliant of God's help, Waliullah bin Abdurrahim al Umari of Delhi—may God foster him, his parents and his elders!—declares that these few pages entitled *The Sacred Knowledge of the Higher Functions of the Mind* are concerned with investigating the real nature of the following:

> The Heart
> The Intellect
> The Self
> The Spirit
> The Secret
> The Concealed
> The Deeply Concealed
> The Pure Intellect
> The Ego

In addition, the correct method of refining each of the above is suggested.

The sole purpose of this discourse is to deal with those

questions pertaining to ecstatic intuition and mystical revelation. It does not come within the scope of the traditional and speculative sciences.

Chapter One

THE KNOWLEDGE OF THE HIGHER FUNCTIONS

In endowing them with the knowledge of the higher functions, God has given later Sufis an invaluable balancing factor. The better one is acquainted with such faculties, the better one is able to refine them; and whoever is ablest in discerning their various characteristics is also the ablest guide for seekers of that knowledge.

To illustrate the difference between someone who possesses the knowledge of these faculties and those people who may have devoted the whole of their lives to mysticism without ever having gained any of this knowledge, we might compare the former to a physician, skilled in the diagnosis of various types of illness, who knows their causes, their symptoms, the methods of treatment, and all the rules which the ancients evolved after long, protracted experience. To continue the analogy, someone who lacks such knowledge is like an unqualified physician who merely prescribes some medicine or other on the strength of his own defective experience and incomplete understanding.

Whoever is acquainted with the higher faculties is like a guide who has spent a lifetime wandering in the wilderness and has learnt each hill and dale, each path across it, whether it be well-worn or as yet untrodden. A number of mystics, however, either through adversity or the intensity of their desire, reached such a pitch of desperation, that they roamed hither and thither in the desert, without any clear notion either of their objective or of the path to be followed. As a result a great many perished; but some of them actually attained their goal and eventually returned to their native land. There each of them related his own partial account of the journey. Their audience were merely disappointed by their contradictory reports, and annoyed to discover that none of these wanderers could remove the contradictions or explain exactly where everything on the journey was located.

Briefly then, if you wish to know the path taken by those who have reached the stage of establishment and have become heirs to the prophetic endowment, it is important that you should realize that this is not possible without a knowledge of these faculties. Likewise, if you wish to travel on the straight path, avoiding all irrelevant detours and useless suffering, such knowledge is equally indispensable.

The knowledge of the higher faculties is an immense blessing which has been bestowed upon recent times. 'It is the bounty of God, bestowed upon us and upon mankind—yet most men are not grateful.'[1]

Contemporary exponents of the path of remembrance and effort, which has been handed down to them by their forbears, may be divided into two distinct categories.

First there is the type of person who experiences a longing to walk on the path leading to God. He therefore begins to travel along it as he sees fit, and finally reaches a stage with which he feels satisfied. Eventually he shows signs of being able to give guidance; so that seekers of truth turn to him, and he accordingly guides them towards the stage which he himself has reached. At this point he is under the impression that this is the only stage to aim for, and that there is no perfection other than this. The disciples of such a guide concentrate exclusively on this path, and place all their reliance on it. Most of them have only one point of reference. For example, they may be connected through their longing and anxiety, or in the same spirit as Uways al-Qarni[2]; or else the link may be

---

[1] Qur'an 12.38.
[2] Uways al-Qarni was a contemporary of the Prophet Muhammad, though the two men never met. The allusion is probably to his proverbial asceticism, and perhaps also to the notion found in John 20: 'Happy are they who never saw me and yet have found faith.'

their affinity with the inferior angels, or the idea of unity or purity, or their attachment to the visionary transports induced by constantly repeated prayers. In such cases, however, only one of their faculties becomes refined through the relationship, while the rest remain unpurified. Such people with only one faculty purified could be likened to someone whose face was half white and half black, since 'they have mixed good actions with bad ones'.[3] Most of them do not observe Holy Law, but say that such things as it enjoins are merely the outward shell of the Law, whereas they have understood its kernel of reality.

The second category of teacher of the path consists of persons of such perfection that the universal administration has appointed them to be guides to the people. Through their agency the community is united and disciplined, and God's purpose is made manifest. They are inspired with the vision of what has to be done, and they in turn transmit these requirements to their disciples, who then pass them on from father to son. Thus it is on this great path along which thousands travel. Spiritual guides such as these have mapped out the way correctly; they have prescribed a cure for every disease and suggested a remedy for every hardship. However, if their followers fail to understand the science of higher faculties, they are bound to suffer many setbacks, some of which are listed below.

In many disciples one faculty is by nature very strong, while the others happen to be very weak. Now if such people blindly begin to carry out exercises with the object of training and refining all the faculties simultaneously, then an extremely long time will be required even for the dominant faculty to be purified, regain strength, come to the boil and show manifest signs of its purification, thus enabling the seeker to reach the desired stage. But if the seeker were to strengthen the faculty which is innately strong, and purify the others only summarily, then the objective could very quickly be achieved, and he would

[3] Qur'an 9.102

reach the desired stage without delay. The final goal, which is reached after passing through a number of stages and undergoing a number of annihilations, is in fact attained thanks to the faculty which is by nature very strong.

A whole series of different states and numerous forms of annihilation and permanence dawn upon the seeker, and as a result he is unable to identify each state with its corresponding faculty. His consequent bewilderment leads him to suppose that he has not gained anything, and that everything which he has experienced up to this point has merely been the deceptions of the devil. Because of this he is constantly plunged in grief and depression, and may even give up the search. But if he could learn to trace the origin of every state and every annihilation and permanency back to a particular faculty, then he would be able to cast off his depression and grief.

The seeker observes the states of various saints, and finds discrepancies in their words and states. As a result of this he is prey to doubts. Sometimes his attention is drawn to this man's state, sometimes to that—with the ultimate consequence that he abandons the activity. Alternatively, he studies a particular person through and through to his utmost limits, and then comes to the conclusion that this is all there is to the path. The truth is, however, that the variation in the states and words and ultimate limits of the various saints is simply the result of the strengths and weaknesses of the faculties in their own particular natures.

In the work which is carried out subsequent to understanding the ultimate purpose, a little effort will serve where previously a great deal of effort would have been needed. The seeker will see the benefits of it every day, and will begin to think deeply and perceptively about it. This in turn will widen his scope. In short the enhancements accruing from the knowledge of these faculties are too many to mention. This scant résumé must suffice to indicate the wealth that is there.

Chapter Two

THE NATURE OF THE SOUL

The exposition of the true nature and properties of the higher faculties depends in turn on an understanding of the true nature of the soul. The latter question belongs to the science of reality[1] rather than to the science of behaviour. The Law-giver, Muhammad, gave no indications concerning the science of reality; he merely gave information about the science of behaviour and the purification of the self. Be that as it may, it is well known that both Arabs and non-Arabs alike are well-acquainted with the former concept, and that there is hardly a group that is not forever talking about the science of reality. The Holy Prophet merely taught these illustrious sciences in general terms to his followers, and firmly forbade any portrayal of them in depth. This has been the practice of all the prophets.

It should never be thought, however, that it is beyond the power of man to fathom these sciences. That is not the case; but the fact of the matter is that the disclosure of these sciences is not really in the interests of ordinary people. Thus it might even seem better for us also to keep silence on this subject and to treat the seen as if it were unseen. But Sufis have differed greatly on this point; and it has always been in their nature relentlessly to pursue this problem. If, as we have indicated, the science of higher faculties is based on the question of the real nature of the soul, then a genuine necessity arises; and, as is well known, necessity can render lawful the unlawful.

By soul we mean that entity which, when it is associ-

---

[1] Mysticism.

ated with the body, is the source of the latter's life, and when divorced from it is the cause of its death.

Let us consider the real nature of the soul. It should be borne in mind that it is composed of three parts.

First there is the subtle substance arising from the fine vapours of the various elements in digested food. It possesses the capacity for nutrition, growth and sense-perception. This is referred to as the breathing soul, the natural soul, or the airy body. It permeates flesh and bones like the fire in charcoal or the scent in a rose. It is by virtue of this part that the soul is connected to the body. Just as the body tastes death when severed from the soul, the latter suffers a similar agony when separated from the body.

The original source of this subtle vapour is in the heart, brain and liver. It arises from the agitation of the blood in the heart. Physicians observe it when the blood becomes thick or thin, pure or impure and increases or decreases. Through experimentation they have discovered the effects of these various states, and proceed with treatment accordingly.

Should the connection be interrupted, death ensues. The dead man is then like a tree which has been cut off from its roots: the systems of nutrition and renewal have been destroyed. However, the dry body of the tree takes a long time to disintegrate and decompose. Similarly, the connection between the rational soul and this subtle vapour remains intact even after death, with the latter persisting unimpaired in the form of the physical body. With the passage of time, however, it begins to disintegrate little by little.

The second part is the rational soul. When a date-stone is planted in the earth, it is encompassed on all sides by small particles of water, air and earth. By virtue of the power which God has placed in it, the date-stone absorbs these particles into itself and transforms them in the process of its own specific and regulated growth. Eventually leaves and shoots appear, and these are at length followed by flowers and fruit. Finally it begins to weaken and is ultimately destroyed. Now when we consider how every single date-stone can control its own independent growth, and how every tree has its own distinct pattern, then we find our reason compelled to acknowledge the existence of a soul possessing the requisite faculties. Likewise, when the male semen and female ovulation combine in the womb, then the woman's soul begins to work on the mixture, until eventually the various organs, the heart, liver and brain come into being, and finally the airy soul is breathed into it. In each of the above cases there are both visible and invisible processes at work: the component particles are rearranged in accordance with a new form with correspondingly different properties.

Similarly there is a soul governing the human order, which gives rise to such attributes in man as a universal outlook and the five faculties, with all their ramifications. This is known as the rational soul. Each individual soul—and indeed every soul in general—is merely a bubble on the ocean of the universal soul, and this we shall now describe in some detail.

People of intuition have come to realize that there is one soul in the universe which is absolute ruler of all that the universe comprises. Every single process in heaven and earth takes place according to the requirements of that soul, which is known as the universal soul. Seen in the perspective of the specific actions which it initiates, it is called universal nature; and the organic structure which this soul requires for itself is called the universal expediency. The various elemental, vegetable, animal and cosmic souls in the universe are all like the constituent organs and members of a body. All are subsumed in one collective soul; all are subject to a single plan. It is that very soul which is both manifest and hidden in all the multifarious forms and states of creation. Gas becomes liquid, liquid becomes gas: in either case the universal soul remains intact; it is merely that in one state it is hidden, while in the other it manifests itself. This universal soul is the fundamental reality of the rational soul. When conditions permit—and indeed require it—the rational soul in its individual manifestation firmly attaches itself to the universal soul. Then, as a result of losing itself in the universal soul, the rational soul achieves the annihilation of its spiritual existence.

The third part is the angelic soul. Inherent in the universal soul are faculties able to contain the form of everything that is to be, even before it actually comes into existence. This is just like the human capacity to visualize a desired action in the mind before that action is made manifest in the external world. In a sense, the square which exists in our mind is the same as the one which comes into existence in the outside world. Similarly it can be said that the form which lies hidden in the faculties of the universal soul is precisely the same form as that which is now to be seen in the world of phenomena.

Thus, long before the actual creation of humanity, when God conceived the intention to create the human race, he created the generalized form of the human species within the faculties of the universal soul. After the lapse of a lengthy period of time, that generalized form received fresh enhancement from the source of divine bounty; in consequence of which that single form appeared in a multiplicity of forms. For the sake of analogy, let us suppose that the sun is reflected in a mirror, and that round that mirror a whole variety of mirrors of every size and colour are placed. Clearly, the form of the sun will be reflected in each one of them. Thus, in one sense, all those forms have an independent existence; while in another sense they all partake of existence solely by virtue of the generalized form: for had it not been there, neither would they have been. We may thus compare each one of these reflected forms to the soul of a single individual.

And so, much later, as a result of further enhancement, the archetypal form descends into lower levels of energy. When the airy soul is breathed into the human body, the universal soul disappears in one aspect, only to reappear in another, more limited aspect, which receives the name of rational soul. The two aspects are intimately united—in the same way that a physical rectangular body is united with the conceptualized form of a rectangular body.

It is on account of this part of the soul that a man is able to be present in the heavenly fold of the world to come, and his deeds are registered in the heavenly records. If he performs a good deed, then a white spot appears on that parallel form; while an evil deed produces a black spot. In the next world the body and its parallel form are united; and as a result of this, one's bodily form will clearly proclaim the record of one's deeds.

In trying to understand the various parts of the soul, it is important also to realize that every part has its own separate properties. In addition to this, each combination of parts has further distinct properties of its own. The soul of man is governed by these properties both in this life and the life to come.

The characteristic property of the airy soul is to reside in the material world and gather sustenance from the elements. The airy soul is found in one of the following three states.

First, it may be ruled and driven by the limbs and organs of the body. Here it functions in a manner which accords entirely with their nature and conditioning; and it is completely submerged in them. The soul in this state is known as the animal soul.

Alternatively it may avoid total submersion in the characteristics of the limbs and organs, and come instead under the influence of those characteristics which are connected with the heart and the brain. It may either be that the limbs and organs fulfil and complete these latter characteristics, and are in fact a pre-condition of them; or else it may be that these characteristics are complete in themselves, and that the actions of the limbs and organs are merely their necessary expression. In either case the soul in question is known as the human soul.

Thirdly, there are a number of means whereby the airy soul may be brought under control and subjection, in which case it becomes the angelic soul. The characteristic property of this soul is that it remains in the presence of the holy spirit, which is established in the heavenly fold. The angelic soul maintains this link at all times, and is firmly established in the exalted assembly, where it may effectively express itself according to its capacity. It is as a result of this that the mysterious and secret intimations of celestial souls are disclosed within the heart of man. In fact the whole basis of the reward of the next world lies in the attraction which this part of the soul feels towards the heavenly fold. If within the airy soul there are attributes which are suited to that place, then the individual will find ease and comfort there; but if there are attributes which bear no relation to that place, then he will be overwhelmed by fear and shame.

An analogy for the close bond between this airy soul and the sublime soul would be the fusion in quicksilver of the properties of metal and liquid, which are bound together in a knot so tight as to be impossible to untie. It is still possible nonetheless to discern the flow of a liquid and the mass of a metal. Similarly the sublime soul and the airy soul are so strongly bonded, that it is extremely difficult to separate one from the other. Wherever one of them is drawn the other is inevitably drawn also. Whenever one of them experiences pleasure or pain, so also in consequence does the other.

The characteristic property of the rational soul in relation to the airy soul is to combine and integrate the various parts of the latter—just as we found in the case of the vegetable soul, which lends a particular shape to the various parts of a tree, and closely combines them in such a way that even if the tree were to be severed from its roots, it would take a long time for the component parts to separate once more. In the same way the rational soul connects up the various component parts of the airy soul into a single constitution. Now if the airy soul should be cut off by death from this body of flesh and blood, and the system of nutrition and procreation should thus break down completely, the airy soul still survives—as long as the rational soul remains intact to manage it. In fact the airy soul comprises a number of faculties which remain intact, such as the common sense, volition and the imaginative and retentive faculties. In the same way, firmly established characteristics, as well as constantly renewed intentions, persist unimpaired in their original condition. The eyes and the ears may be lost, but the common sense is there to do their work. During his long sojourn in the world, man uses his ears and eyes for perception, and becomes thoroughly accustomed to this state of affairs; but after he has become separated from these organs, the common sense begins to serve the purpose of both ears and eyes—either by virtue of the rational soul, or else due to the universal expediency, which can supersede an individual's particular objectives. The merest attention from the source of all bounty is sufficient to cause visible and audible forms to flow into it; just as, when a man considers a set of premises, a logical deduction flows into his faculty of understanding.

The fundamental function of the rational soul is to lose itself in the universal soul, and by a process of osmosis receive the impulse of the greater selfhood. Through the intermediary of the angelic soul it is able to receive the inspiration of the angels and experience the vision of the heavenly fold. If a man's airy soul becomes subject to his angelic soul, then he becomes like one of the exalted assembly, or one of the angels of the lower assembly.

It is in the combinations between the airy soul and the two subtler parts (the rational and angelic souls) that the five higher faculties are created. The secret circumstances of their birth are these: since both rational and angelic souls rely for their subsistence on the airy soul, they both bring their love and affection to bear on it. As a result, in the process of diversifying the faculties of the airy soul, the abundant grace of the subtler parts is in its turn further enhanced.

The faculty which has its basis in the liver is known as the carnal self; the faculty which has its basis in the physical heart, and which is the bearer of the individual's qualities, is in fact called the heart; while the faculty whose basis is in the brain and whose characteristic property is to apprehend concepts, whether imaginary or objectively real, is known as the intellect. The self, the heart and the intellect all reside in the airy soul. However, the latter receives the enhancement of the two subtle parts, just as the ground near to a spring receives its freshness and moisture—or just as the body receives refreshment from the liver by means of the lymphatic system.

Although each one of these faculties is originally created from all three parts, the self has an affinity with the airy soul, the intellect with the heavenly soul, and the heart with the rational soul. This is why the ancients described the heart as the human faculty and called the intellect the tongue of the soul.

When the seeker gains some freedom from the domination of the airy soul, he then has to deal with the two subtler parts. At this stage his heart becomes his spirit and his intellect becomes his secret faculty.

The difference between the heart and the spirit is this: the heart is a function of the airy soul which has arisen from the depths of the physical body; but it is governed by the grace of the two subtle parts and is permeated by them. By spirit we mean that the two subtle parts, intimately united, have clothed themselves in the finest garb of the airy soul, on which they totally depend.

The difference between the intellect and the secret faculty is that the former is a function of the airy soul; its location is in the brain, but it is governed by the grace of the two subtle parts and permeated by them. By secret faculty we mean that the two subtle parts are bonded tightly together and dressed in the finest garment of the airy soul, on which they depend.

For this reason the spirit is subtler than the heart, and the secret is brighter than the intellect. The function of the heart is to experience love and longing, while that of the spirit is to experience intimacy. The function of the intellect is to gain certitude, while that of the secret is to attain beatific vision. However, there are many gradations.

When the seeker has become completely free of the airy soul, he has to deal with the two subtle parts, which are as intimately conjoined as the liquid and metallic properties of quicksilver. At this point the seeker's state will come under one of the following headings.

The angelic soul may exert its attraction, in which case the seeker will lose himself in the holy spirit, and pass through annihilation in it to permanence and recollection of himself. This is the prophetic inheritance.

Alternatively, the rational soul may exert its attraction, and then the seeker will be annihilated in the greater selfhood, attain permanence and come to himself again. This is the stage of major sainthood.

Thirdly, the seeker may achieve a balanced combination of both these stages. This stage is known as union of union. There are two ways in which the person who attains to this stage may be remembered. Sometimes he is remembered from the standpoint of the universal soul; and the impulse of the greater selfhood descends and permeates him. At other times he is remembered from the standpoint of the holy spirit; and the impulses of the exalted assembly descend into him by a process analogous to osmosis. It is to this third type that I myself aspire to belong.

Chapter Three

THE MANIFEST FACULTIES

We shall now discuss the purification of the manifest faculties according to the requirements of practical wisdom. The human faculty may be subdivided into three branches: the heart, the self and the intellect. All three of these faculties are mentioned in the Traditions of the Prophet Muhammad. From this source we are able to gather that desire and the pursuit of pleasure are the attributes of the self; forming the intention to carry out a particular action, entertaining feelings of love and hatred, showing courage or cowardice, etc.—these are the characteristics of the heart; understanding and knowledge, and the capacity to decide what has to be decided—these are the qualities which are attributed to the intellect.

The faculties of the rational soul have been divided by the wise into three categories: natural faculties, animal faculties and intelligent faculties. These have been located respectively in the liver, the physical heart and the brain. All of this has received detailed discussion in their books, and this topic is one of their most noted preoccupations. However, it is not the concern of this present work to discuss these matters.

The basic function of the self is to look after the carnal needs and to pursue whatever is pleasurable. In addition it has to maintain the constitution of the body in accordance with the latter's requirements; and it has to repel what the body, by its nature, requires to be repelled. Hunger and thirst, fatigue and pain, the sexual urge, excretory needs—all of these are connected with the self and form the absolute necessities for the continuance of life. However, by dint of hard exercise the nature of the self can be changed and it can be extricated from its own inherent constitution.

The function of the heart is to show anger, shame, fear, courage, generosity, avarice, love and hatred. Everyone knows for certain why he dislikes a particular thing, and why his heart all but bursts with the agitated desire to repel it, and why his spirits seem almost on the point of leaving his body, and why his veins dilate and his skin becomes red. Similarly, in times of fear, he knows why his heart trembles, and his spirits seem to retreat within his body, and why his face becomes pale and his mouth goes dry. It is in this way that the characteristics of the heart may be assessed.

The function of the intellect is to recollect the things of the past and plan for the things of the future.

Each one of us personally experiences all of these realities. In one sense these three categories are separate from each other, while in another sense they are united together. The cause of their differentiation is the fact that the rational soul, which has penetrated the airy and the natural souls, at one and the same time both directs and depends on them. These souls have different locations, constitutions and faculties.

There is a type of man whose natural powers—his digestion, his power to catch and hold, his sexual energy—are all extremely strong; but as far as the qualities of the heart and the perceptiveness of the intellect are concerned, he is nothing but a dull-minded idiot. Anger, courage, fear and shame are slow to appear in him and disappear in no time. His recollection of the past is extremely feeble, as is his capacity to plan for the future and decide what is good or bad. Such a person may be likened to the vegetables.

Then there is the man of courage and zeal, generosity and authority; and in these qualities he surpasses his fellows; but in his natural and intellectual powers he hardly possesses a tenth of what others possess. He is like the stable animals and the wild beasts.

Again there is the type of man who distinguishes

himself from those around him by his capacity to retain what he has heard, and his ability to adopt the right course; but he has no share whatsoever in the natural energies of those of the heart. Hence he is comparable to the lower angels.

When we examine the condition of various individuals, we find that they are deficient in certain types of energy and strong in others. The different locations of these energies and the varying forms of disorder to which different individuals are subject lead necessarily to the conclusion that there are different kinds of energy.

We have already discussed the cause of their differentiation; the cause of their unity lies in the fact that, although the rational soul directs these various categories, it is itself fundamentally a single, undivided entity. These three types of energy are like fountains gushing forth from a single source, or streams belonging to a single river. However, the action of one would not be complete without the support of the others.

Unless the self obeys the heart, the veins of the throat will not swell, nor will the spirits be aroused; and unless the intellect displays to the heart the image of some threat, hatred and the desire for revenge cannot arise. Similarly, knowledge which is not accompanied by the firm intention of the heart can simply be called talking to oneself. If a mental perception lacks the conviction which sense perceptions can lend to it, it is bound to be lame and distorted. Likewise the self without the support of the intellect or the heart is as helpless as a three-month-old baby; such a person is unable to muster confidence, firmness and strength from within himself.

And so in order to effect a combination of these disparate yet unified parts, a sort of lymphatic system extends between them and links them all together, with the result that each one communicates its influence to the other. In this way a whole variety of characteristics and qualities are created. A full exposition of this point would call for a major elaboration; however, the following considerations are all that is necessary for the purposes of this present discourse.

If both the heart and the intellect are subservient to the self, then a great many vices will result. The self in that state is generally known as the animal self. Such acts, for example, as indulging in sexual pleasures, gazing at and caressing one's beloved, cause the heart to follow suit; they arouse an inclination for the loved one, and fill the heart with love. At the same time they compel the intellect to summon up the image and memory of the beloved and to find ways and means to effect a union. All of this is called love. In the same way, indulgence in delicious food and drink causes the heart and the intellect to follow suit. With a little attention such patterns are easily recognized.

If both the self and the intellect happen to obey the heart, a number of different vices will appear. The self in that condition is called the aggressive self. Besides violent anger, a whole array of other vices arise in the aggressive self. For example, if the heart has an underlying spirit which is coarse without being evil, then the man possessing such a heart will seek to dominate those around him. This characteristic is innate in the heart, which is why the self lends its support. In an activity such as wrestling it summons up fresh strength and rouses the man's inborn spirits to lend assistance. Supposing it is necessary to abstain for a period from eating or drinking or marriage, the heart raises no objections and does not rise in revolt. The intellect, too, shares in the action of the heart, and for its sake hits on many an elegant stratagem and plan for the future.

If both the heart and the self are governed by the intellect, then praiseworthy qualities will result. The self in this condition is known as the serene self. For example, when a man comes to realize through his intellect that his happiness lies in performing good actions, while bad actions will only bring him misery, then his self no longer goes against or objects to the command of the intellect;

and his heart, too, begins to show love and desire for what reason requires. It often happens that a man of abundant intellect thinks of some desirable worldly or religious objective. Then however much his heart may dislike certain aspects of it, and even though sweet pleasures may meanwhile be slipping through his hands, still his heart and self do not disobey his intellect.

There is a type of man who is so strong in his heart, that when he becomes angry or jealous, or is overtaken by worry or shame, his self ceases to function. He feels neither hunger nor thirst, and lacks even the strength to digest and evacuate. No matter how much his intellect may chide him and tell him that there is no point in showing anger or worrying, it is impossible for him to escape the dictates of his heart.

Then there is the type of man whose self is strong and who is given over to sexual indulgence and eating delicious food. Even though the fear of the punishment meted out for such actions may occur to him, and his intellect may vividly portray the abuse, humiliation and hatred which await him, he is just like a male ass falling upon a female, or one that is bent on fodder; and he takes no account at all of lash or cudgel, so engrossed is he in what he is doing. All of which makes people of sense realize that every part is busy dominating as well as supporting the other. The intellect may occasionally understand the baseness of the action and its evil consequences; but it cannot put its orders into effect.

Sometimes the intellect may absorb knowledge calculated to further the drive for conquest. To this end it then begins to think out beneficial contingencies and effective plans, thus retreating from its former convictions. This is a vice which is extremely hard to eradicate.

It sometimes happens that the heart is filled with desire for a sweetheart, and yet the necessary sexual energy is lacking. Or the heart may be filled with contemptuous and vengeful thoughts, and yet the arm is bereft of all strength. Occasionally in such cases the self comes to the aid of the heart and pours in renewed vigour which was lacking before. This vice is also extremely difficult to eradicate and avoid.

Such characteristics as these are like natural bodily needs, whose total eradication is absolutely impossible. Lord knows, they may be temporarily concealed while severe exercises are being performed; but no sooner are these exercises discontinued than they appear once more. In fact the purification of these characteristics can only consist in this: that one uses them in their proper place, contenting oneself with what is necessary and avoiding excess.

To recapitulate briefly: the self is located in the liver, the heart is located in the physical heart, and the intellect is located in the brain. The animal self permeates the whole body, but is firmly rooted in the liver; the aggressive self is present throughout the whole body, but it is firmly rooted in the heart; and the serene self also pervades the entire body, but it is firmly rooted in the brain.

It should be borne in mind that God has created two distinct types of energy in man. One comprises the earthly, human energies, collectively called animal energy, by means of which man performs the actions of the animals and is thus counted as one of their number. The other type of energy comprises the angelic faculties, by means of which man carries out the work of angels and is hence regarded as one of their number. The meaning and purpose of the purification of the self is that the angelic energy should gain control over the animal energy, and that the characteristics of the former should come into prominence, whilst those of the animals should remain in abeyance, with a corresponding decrease in their effects.

The question of purification is more in the province of Holy Law than of natural philosophy, though the latter does have some bearing on it. Since there are so many variations in the three basic types of human being, the means of purification for each of them will also differ; and thus the scope of this topic becomes enormous. It should be remembered, too, that the stages of purification of these three types are also different: each has its own form and pattern. This is why the matter has become obscure and bewildering to a number of seekers, who are unable to understand how to effect unity among all the multifarious forms and patterns of the three types. However, the people of establishment do recognize and distinguish all the different forms and patterns, and are well-acquainted with the method of achieving a systematic and consistent unity. 'And God speaks the truth and shows the way.'

Chapter Four

HOLY LAW AND THE MANIFEST FACULTIES

We shall now discuss the purification of the body and the three manifest faculties according to the requirements of the spiritual method which God revealed without distinction to all conditions of humanity, and which is currently known as the Law. The first stage in the purification of these faculties consists in turning away from one's inborn nature and turning towards the Law.

If you are seeking to understand the reality of the Law, then you are probably aware that human beings were in the grip of the commanding self. The devil had prevailed in them to such an extent, and they were reduced to such a state, that if they had died in that condition they would have incurred the punishment of the grave and judgment day. With the exception of a handful of people, no one living at that time would have found deliverance. Almighty God, the ruler of heaven and earth, in his infinite mercy showed favour to this handful of dust, in that he allowed mankind to participate in his universal administration. Sometimes the universal administration assumes the form of a specific dispensation. Eventually someone from among the people was selected, and into his heart was poured the knowledge of what was needed to remedy the general malady. He was then inspired to convey that knowledge to the people and to make them follow it whether they liked it or not. The remedy proposed as a cure for this malady is called the Law.

This remedy only took into account man's specific form and general characteristics—not the particular capacities of certain individuals. Its final purpose is to achieve deliverance from the wrongs done among the people of this world and from the punishment of the grave and the day of judgment. Its purpose is not to enable man to achieve the stages of annihilation and permanency in each of his faculties, or to attain for himself the rank of absolute permanency and complete establishment.

This and this alone is what is intended in the words which you have received from the Holy Prophet: namely, that men should avoid wrongdoing and act in such a way as to escape the punishment of the grave and judgment day. Whoever thinks otherwise has not understood the Prophet's aims, strategies, commands and prohibitions. If indeed he spoke of those other objectives, and described the benefits of all those perfections, this was done in some other way.

To make an analogy, the sun ripens the melon without knowing that there is a melon seed sown in the earth; nor does the melon know that its ripening has been effected by the sun. In the same way the Source of all bounty has created universal souls for universal purposes; and they are able to perfect souls that are defective, without so much as a word passing between them.

Certain intelligent people are indeed able to recognize those other blessings, and by way of subjective association they can infer allusions to such things in the words and sayings of the Holy Prophet. However, from what I have learnt of him in this respect, I do not think that he himself intended the novel and constantly changing meanings which men have inferred from what he said. The natural intention of his words, which is like the tendency of fire to rise and earth to fall, is an altogether different matter. Thus, by making a distinction between the natural intention and one which is a subsequent innovation, we may avoid the confusion caused by those mystics who have been careless in this respect. I must therefore ask them to excuse me from agreeing to their hair-splittings.

Briefly, the substance of the system is this: there are two types of energy found in man: the angelic and the animal. Each type has its own supporting characteristics. What is required is that man should adorn himself with the angelic properties, so that the angelic faculties may become stronger, and so that the animal faculties may be trained in their ways and take on their colouring. However, this should not take place in such a way that the animal faculties become divested of their own nature, qualities and taste, or that their reality is turned upside-down.

God has drawn man's attention towards the cultivation of four cardinal virtues. If you think carefully, you will find that all kinds of goodness are merely an elaboration of these four virtues; conversely, all types of sin are merely an elaboration of their opposite characteristics. These four virtues are precisely the ones which all the prophets have exhorted the people to imbibe. There can be no question of any change or abrogation with regard to these virtues. If there is any difference in what the various Lawgivers say about them, this is only a matter of their outward form, not their real substance.

The first virtue is purity: through this, man is related to the angels. The second is humility, by means of which man acquires an affinity with the exalted assembly. The third is generosity: by cultivating this quality, man wipes out the stains left by base human nature, such as the actions of animality and lust still firmly rooted in his rational soul. The fourth virtue is justice: it is through justice that a man may be pleasing in the sight of the exalted assembly, may gain favour with it and receive its mercy and blessings.

The strategy of the Law with regard to the foregoing is developed in two directions. The first involves effecting a reformation through good deeds, the abandonment of the major sins, and the establishment of the marks of true religion. For these three things the observances and limits are laid down, and all followers of the Law are required to abide by them. This is the outward form of the Law and is called Islam. The second direction consists in the purification of the various selves through the reality of the four virtues, and passing from these forms of goodness to the splendours which they contain, and progressing from the mere outward abstention from sin to a repudiation of its very essence. This is the inward form of the Law and it is called charity.

Now when the Law had prepared the people to adopt this strategy, and had brought them to the point, willingly or otherwise, of putting it into practice, individuals differed widely in the extent to which they accepted it, on account of their different dispositions and vocations. They thus inevitably fell into one of three categories—a point to which the Holy Qur'an alludes:

> Then we have given
> the Book for inheritance
> to such of our servants
> as we have chosen:
> but there are among them
> some who wrong their own souls,
> some who follow a middle course,
> and some who are, by God's leave,
> foremost in good deeds:
> that is the highest grace.[1]

In amplification of this we can say that when the angelic energy is in conflict with the animal energy, the outcome is bound to be one of three situations.

Either the animal energy will prevail, and the angelic energy will be subdued to such an extent as not to be in evidence at all—except on certain occasions, and even then it will be far from pleased with its own particular attributes. If a man is dominated by his own evil and harmful actions, he is a scoundrel; but if his evil and corrupt characteristics become even stronger, then such a person is called a hypocrite, since his actions are never free from hypocrisy.

Alternatively, the angelic energy may have the animal energy firmly by the neck, but the latter still has its hands and feet free to continue the struggle. As long as the angelic energy does not slacken its grip and withdraw from the fight, such a person is called a 'companion of the

[1] Qur'an 35.32 (from the translation by Yusuf Ali).

right-hand side'. There are two possible explanations for the persistence of animal energies in this situation: on the one hand, either the aggressive energy or the intellectual energy may be inherently weak; such a person may perform many good actions, but the desired benefit of such actions cannot be realized. On the other hand these energies may have been created in a sound condition within him; and yet he has failed to perform many good actions, having become dominated by his concern for his daily bread.

The third situation is found when the angelic energy finally achieves victory and holds the animal soul in close captivity, shattering its base desires and keeping it permanently starved. Such a person is called 'foremost of those who are near to God'. In the case of this latter individual two things are essential: first, his aggressive and intellectual energies must have been created in a sound condition; and second, his intellect must have been purified by the true articles of faith and must have managed to seize and subjugate the resolve of the heart. This power of resolve, which we name the aggressive faculty, is then able to control the self. In this way the individual becomes entirely worthy of nearness to God.

Here it is necessary to give a clear exposition of the signs which characterize these three types, and also to mention the rules which the Lawgiver laid down for the purification within each of them of the three faculties. Then we can make a distinction between the form of purification which is termed reformation, and another form of purification which has as its outcome an actual change in the person's nature. We can also mention the distinction which the Lawgiver himself made between these two forms.

In discussing the outward form of the Law, which is given the name of Islam, we have in mind the bodily faculty. As is stated in the Qur'an:

> The desert Arabs say, 'We believe.'
> Tell them: 'You do not believe,

> but merely say that you have surrendered;
> faith has not yet entered
> into your hearts.'²

What this means is that there is only an outward acknowledgement and performance of what is required. The truth concerning this faculty is as follows. The heart, the intellect and the self, in their capacity of maintaining the limbs and organs of the body, merging in with them and causing them to perform their various functions, collectively receive the label of bodily faculty. In other words, the term corresponds to that state where heart, intellect and self are completely absorbed in the service of the bodily limbs and organs. As an analogy of this, I was once shown a camel on the verge of death: only a few last breaths remained in it. All of its faculties had become very weak, and no energy remained in it except to walk along in the file of camels to which it was attached. It continued walking along, until finally it dropped down dead. This camel, so I was told, was lost in the bodily faculty. It is this faculty that is generally under discussion in the Law; and it will be in the light of the functioning of this faculty that reward or punishment will be meted out in the next world.

Thus the remedy fixed in the Law for dealing with a scoundrel is merely an external one: he is held in confinement whether he likes it or not, so that he has to desist from his crime. For example, the observation by men and women of the segregation of the sexes was originally prescribed so that they might not see each other; and thus, as long as people abided by it, no sin could take place. Not only was there a deterrent punishment for fornication, but men were also forbidden such behaviour as might lead to fornication and thus ultimately to punishment, such as looking at a woman's beauty or freely mixing with women. Similarly the preparation and sale of wine was prohibited, and a deterrent punishment was fixed for drunkenness. All of this was done in such a way that if

² Qur'an 49.14.

there had really been a caliphate in the true sense of that word,[3] these sins which are rampant in the world would by now have been totally eradicated. However, it is not the concern of this present book to discuss this subject.

The following are the three basic types of hypocrite.

First, there is the type of person who is ruled by his physical energy and carnal self. Both his heart and his intellect are subservient to these, and his aggressive and perceptive selves lend them their support. By nature such a person goes wherever he likes without the permission of law or reason, and does whatever he wishes. He becomes involved in love affairs, even though reason and Law forbid it. If he is held up to shame by conventional standards, he pays this no heed whatsoever; as if he had some kind of certificate exempting him from the Law and from popular retribution. He always keeps in mind some excuse or other for his behaviour, and uses this to drive out any thought for the Law, which may be lurking like a last grain of faith in the back of his mind. In the Holy Qur'an God describes such a hypocrite as deceitful: 'They try to deceive God, but he deceives them.'[4] Elsewhere there is reference to their 'twisted breasts'.[5] By breast is meant the knowledge of the breast; and the twisting of it means that the hypocrite covers the thought of truth with the thought of untruth, and changes his knowledge into ignorance.

Sometimes this type of hypocrite sinks even lower than this, and does not take the slightest note of the Law, being entirely satisfied with his unspoken excuse—though at times conflict and contradiction may flare up in his breast. Or he may sink still lower, and, holding firmly to his sense of licence, become totally indifferent to the prohibition of the Law. Occasionally he may sink to the lowest level of all and actually begin to take pride in his sin and try to demonstrate its beauty. In such a case, as God has said: 'Their sin has encompassed them. They are

[3] i.e., a line of succession from the Prophet.
[4] Qur'an 4.142.
[5] Qur'an 11.5.

the companions of fire, and will remain there forever.'[6] We take refuge with God from the actions of our evil selves!

A person of this type plunges himself into such indulgences as gluttony, drinking, playing chess, gaming and setting animals to fight one another. He enjoys ease and fine living, and forever craves splendid clothes and finely decorated houses. The very thought of these things gives him pleasure, and his heart takes delight in seeking them. Even his intellect is likewise engaged in striving for them. He is angry with those who criticize such activities and takes as his friend whoever approves of his pursuits. He shows aversion towards everything which tends to keep him away from his pleasures. Where friendship is concerned, he spends his wealth lavishly and gives freely of himself to help any friend in need. Conversely, if he has occasion to show hatred, he thinks nothing of abusing, striking or even killing the offending person. He may keep a grudge concealed for a long time, but in the end it will come into the open. His intellect uses every possible device to conjure up the image of pleasure, and it thinks up stratagems to obtain it. It removes any obstacles from his path, and grants him licence in anything he might consider himself unable to do.

The second type of hypocrite is one whose aggressive energy is excessive; with the result that his self and his intellect are subservient. Such a person is constantly engaged in gaining dominance over his fellows and revenging himself on those who put up any resistance. He can conceal a grudge for a long time, and is continuously thinking of killing, striking, overthrowing or humiliating his adversaries. He accepts those who defer to him, and seeks to overthrow anyone who happens to be his equal. The slightest word is enough to make him lose his temper and declare that he is not the sort of person who can brook any dishonour or threat. 'Come what may, it's all one to me. Rather hell-fire than dishonour!'—such is his religion. And it is also part of his religion to go to

[6] Qur'an 2.81.

extremes in the pursuit of his honour. In this respect his self obeys him and his intellect assists him. He is prepared to tolerate any hardship if he can thereby give practical expression to his anger. With the greatest ease he devises plans to show his rancour and revenge.

Sometimes, on the other hand, he may be seized with such a degree of friendship for people or attachment to a custom, that he strives valiantly on their behalf, without considering the prohibitions of Law and reason. It is an essential feature of his conduct, so he says, to remain loyal to his friends, and it is an inherent part of his constitution to abide by his own customs. He is not one of those shameless creatures who can change friends and customs from one moment to the next. In the opinion of the uninformed, such people with a marked aggressive drive are truly strong, and superior to those who are driven by lust. However, tastes differ.

The third type of hypocrite is one whose intelligence is confused. Or perhaps his intellect may be sound, but he has nonetheless fallen into some sort of error—such as believing that God has a body, or ascribing human attributes to God, or believing that God does not have any attributes, etc. Or he may entertain doubts concerning the Holy Qur'an or the Holy Prophet or the future life, without ever having gone so far as to be declared an apostate. Alternatively the situation may be that his intelligence has been overrun by dark oppressive thoughts; so that he is no longer convinced about anything and is thus unable to bring his intentions to any sort of conclusion. Or it may be that he has gone too deeply into poetry or mathematics, and thus failed to give sufficiently deep thought to the Law.

Thus there are basically three types of hypocrite; but owing to the fact that the three types may be mixed together in varying combinations depending on the context and the activity in question, there are ultimately innumerable different types. The remedy established by the Lawgiver for these various types of hypocrite is that they should live in such a way that their intellect should control their aggressive self and the latter should control their carnal self. Each of these controls is maintained by appropriate actions.

It is thus necessary for man to believe in the existence of God, who sends messengers, reveals scriptures, decrees what is lawful and what unlawful, rewards the deeds of his servants, and knows both what is manifest and what is hidden. All this God has done as 'a reminder of his blessings for the obedient and his punishment for the disobedient, and of death and what follows thereafter.' He has prescribed actions consonant with this point of view, such as regular prayer and the keeping of fasts, so that when the intellect is eventually convinced of their benefit, the nature of the aggressive self will in turn be duly reformed. Thus the individual will experience the fear of punishment, the hope of reward and the love of God and all his signs. Then the self may devote all its energy to this fear, hope and love, at the same time as subduing the aggressive self and shunning its actions.

God bestowed his favour upon the intellect so that he might converse with it according to its nature. He gave it a certain degree of freedom in order to enable it to understand his attributes and in order to remove its suspicions and doubts. He also bestowed other favours on it, such as empowering it to rule over the aggressive self and deal with it according to its nature, in the light of the fear, hope and love of the Benefactor, retaining those aspects of the aggressive nature which would be of value in eternity. Furthermore he allowed the aggressive self to rule over the animal self and direct such of its activities as were desirable towards the life to come. As a result it became like someone who relinquished immediate gain in favour of the profit of the future life. Basically this method consists in following the natural equilibrium; and thus the often quoted saying is borne out, that art takes after nature. And so the bodily method is for the body to follow nature; while the spiritual method consists in following a strong and balanced self.

To enlarge on this point: all individuals of whatever

species differ from one another; some manifest the specific form completely, while others, owing to inherent physical defects, do not receive every aspect of the inherent imprint. There are even some who are fundamentally at odds with the characteristics of the species. For example, the specific human form requires that sexual desire, anger and courage should appear fully and completely in man—not partially. In some men all these emotions are indeed manifested in a complete form; but in others they are only partially apparent. There are others yet again in whom physical degeneracy has brought about undue timidity and impotence.

Man's internal constitution demands that the intellect should rule over the aggressive self, and the latter should control the carnal self. Let us suppose there is a man on horseback, who has taken a panther with him to go hunting. In such a situation the essential requirement is that the rider should be able to control the panther and that the panther should be able to catch the prey.

Essentially the Law is in accord with a balanced natural disposition. This point is made clear in the tradition in which the Holy Prophet says: 'There is no one who is not born according to nature. It is one's parents who make of one a Jew, a Christian or a Magian. The young of animals are not born with slit ears or noses.'[7]

Thus, if the intellect prevails over the aggressive self and the latter dominates the animal energies, a balanced state is produced in the individual. He may then proceed to fix the suitable course for his animal energies to follow in order to satisfy such needs as eating, drinking, clothing, shelter, marriage, etc.—in such a way that these do not clash or conflict with his intellect nor do they impede his aggressive energy. In this manner the reformation of the animal faculty is achieved.

The individual allows his aggressive faculty to pursue the middle course in life, at the same time as avoiding any disturbance of the animal energies. In this way it cherishes true love for the Almighty—real faith, awe and

[7] Mishkat.

hope in him. Clearly the intellect has an important part to play in both these processes.

Practices have been established by means of which the animal self can be made to obey both the aggressive self and the intellect—such practices as the keeping of fasts and the performance of good acts for the expiation of sins. Here both intellect and aggressive self combine to demand the performance of a particular act, whether the animal self should wish it or not. Similarly a method has been found for the purification of the aggressive energy and this comprises perpetual service and the practice of audition.

The people who follow this course of purification fall into a number of categories:

First, there are those whose heart faculty is well-purified. They are known as 'the trustworthy', 'the martyrs', 'the worshipping devotees'. Friendship with God and with his Prophet, and perpetual service have become their dominant characteristics. All their anger is vented in waging war on the enemies of God.

Then there are those whose carnal faculty is highly purified. They are thus called 'the pious'; and they are entirely engrossed in giving up the charms of this transitory life.

Next come those whose intellectual faculty is very strong. They are accordingly known as 'the firmly rooted in knowledge'.

Then there are people who, though they may not have achieved complete purification, have nonetheless saved themselves from the evil of hypocrisy to a certain extent. These are called 'the companions of the right hand'.

There are yet other types of person, but to enumerate them all would go beyond the scope of this present work.

The Holy Prophet has clearly indicated the characteristics of hypocrites, of those who are near to God, and of the companions of the right hand. For example he has said: 'That person in whom these three things are found is a pure hypocrite: first, when he makes a promise he does not fulfil it; second, when he disputes with someone he becomes abusive; and third, when something is entrusted to him he betrays his trust.'[8]

God, in his glorious Qur'an, has drawn a very vivid picture of these three kinds of person, and has removed the extraneous material which fools had allowed to be mixed into this spiritual method. Thus he prevented men from fasting continuously, and frowned on a life of isolation and seclusion. This was in order that the balance should not be lost on the scales of the spiritual method—between internal constitution and the requirements of a healthy nature. 'This is the decree of God, the Mighty, the Knower.'[9]

---

[8] Bukhari.
[9] Qur'an 36.38.

Chapter Five

THE TEACHING OF JUNAID

According to Junaid of Baghdad, the Lord of the Sufis,[1] the purification of the five faculties is known as the 'way' and 'deep knowledge'.

After the era of the Companions of the Prophet and of those who followed them, there appeared certain people who immersed themselves in Holy Law and showed extreme rigidity in their scrupulous obedience to its injunctions concerning self-mortification and similar matters which they happened to have heard about. Thus, without taking into account the question of proportion, and without making a proper diagnosis of the disease, they proposed one single medicine for every ailment. They maintained that man's only obstacle was his own self, his habits and customs, and that for this reason the utmost effort should be made to tame the fury of both the carnal and the aggressive self.

Accordingly they opted to refrain from sexual contact, delicious food and fine clothing, and in so doing became weak and effete through neglect of the legitimate requirements of the self. Or else they chose a hard and austere way of life, ignoring the comforts enjoyed by city dwellers. They took care, however, to fulfil the minimal necessities of life, and maintained their bodies with a bitter medicine, so to speak. They plunged into introspection with similar zeal and were fond of undertaking journeys. They engaged their minds in such pursuits as would make them completely forget any yearning after pomp, dignity and renown—any desire for power or wealth.

They spent their life in the desert, constantly mindful

[1] Died 910 A.D.

that death, whether natural or violent, was an ever present fact. They had no commerce with the world; nor did the world have any business with them. They trained their mental powers to such an extent that, to the exclusion of all else, they were able to penetrate to the true essence of prayer, without the slightest prompting of the self ever occurring to their minds. In both worship and worldly transactions they made it their aim to steer clear of the controversies of the legists and they turned their back on anything that might cause doubt.

This is the mysticism of the masses: undergoing severe exercises without any due proportion—failing from start to finish to recognize the right path. The first man to lay down rules for this way of life was Harith Muhasibi.[2] In these few words I have given the substance of the views held by this sect.

Through such austerities certain worthy aspirants were creating in themselves a state similar to that of the inferior angels. Some of them were inspired to control the affairs of the people, just as their own lives were in the hands of the inferior angels. Such people were known as the 'changed ones'. There were others, however, who were not inspired in this way; and yet at times certain visionary powers would make an appearance of sorts in them. As a result they would receive mystical revelations, or hear voices from the unseen, or even traverse the earth or walk on water.

The Sufi Master, Junaid, is the first person who went beyond such mystification, and who, by adopting the middle course, was able to place every spiritual exercise where it rightly belonged. Every would-be Sufi who came after him followed in Junaid's footsteps, and is thus under an obligation to him, whether he is aware of it or not.

Abu Talib Makki,[3] who enjoys the same position among the Sufis as is enjoyed by Abu Hanifa among the Imams, explicitly and openly discusses the path of Junaid; however he mixes it together with the path of

---

[2] Died in Baghdad, 857 A.D.
[3] Author of *Quwwat-ul-Qulub*, died 996 A.D.

Muhasibi, since at that period, Sufism had not been entirely purified of such rigid austerity. And God knows best.

Briefly, the path of the Master, Junaid, is based on the purification of the five faculties—namely, the self, the heart, the intellect, the spirit and the secret. There is a particular method of purification for each of them; and they each have their own properties and location in the human body. In Sufi terminology the purification of the self, the heart and the intellect is known as the 'way'; whilst that of the spirit and the secret is termed 'deep knowledge'.

Confusion has arisen at this point as a result of careless interpretation of Sufi teaching. I should like here to point out the principal cause of this confusion once and for all, so that it is not necessary to give a detailed account of it in every chapter.

It should be realized that words such as *ruh* (soul, spirit) and *nafs* (self, soul) are used in a great many senses. For example, sometimes the word 'self' is used to mean the source of life; in this sense the self is synonymous with the soul. Sometimes people use the word self to mean human nature, with its needs for food and drink, etc. On other occasions, when the word self is mentioned, what is meant is the carnal self.

A detailed account of all this has already been given above. As we have seen, human nature rules the heart and the intellect and has enslaved them both, with the result that a great number of vices arise. We name the sum total of these evils the self.

Similarly, when people mention the heart, they are sometimes referring to the cone-shaped lump of flesh; while at other times they intend to convey the idea of a mental faculty, synonymous with the intellect. However, what we mean here by this term is that the spirits of the heart bear such mental attributes as anger and embarrassment; and in this the heart is assisted by both the intellect and the self.

The word 'intellect' sometimes refers to knowledge, or

the faculty which gives rise to knowledge. In this sense, the intellect becomes merely an accidental corporeal property, and not an eternal independent absolute. Elsewhere people speak of the intellect, but really mean the essence of the soul, since its functions include understanding. What we mean by intellect is the perceptive energy which imagines and verifies, so that the heart and the self may follow its lead, and a co-ordinating function may arise in the constitution of the perceptive faculty, to which heart and self lend their support. It has been established in the foregoing investigation that these three faculties pervade the whole body; however, the heart is rooted in the physical heart, the self is rooted in the liver, and the intellect is rooted in the brain.

In the same way, people at times use the word 'spirit' in the sense of the source of life; and sometimes they mean the gentle breeze which wafts through the body of flesh and blood. At other times they use it to refer to the angelic soul, which was created thousands of years before the creation of man. What we mean by the spirit in this context is precisely the heart after it has abandoned its baser impulses, when its affinity with the angelic and rational souls becomes predominant.

Similarly, the 'secret' is not ascribed any particular meaning either in common parlance or in the Law. The word itself indicates concealment; but then each one of the subtle faculties is concealed. This is why people sometimes refer to the intellect and sometimes to the spirit as the secret faculty. What we intend to convey by the term is precisely the intellect after it has given up earthly inclinations and is governed by the impulses of the sublime world, thus attaining to the contemplation of the supreme manifestation. In the course of our investigation it has been established that the spirit faculty is super-corporeal but that its particular domain is the physical heart. The secret faculty is super-corporeal likewise, but its particular sphere is the brain.

Thus, because of variation in the technical terms used by Sufi writers, the intended meaning may not be clear, and the text becomes difficult to understand. For example, when some Sufis expound on one of the states of the heart, they may go very deeply into the subject, and then in the same breath speak of a state of the spirit as if it were an inner dimension of the heart. Again, when they discuss the love of the heart, they may take attachment, intimacy and attraction as its inner aspects; but all of these are states of the spirit, not states of the heart.

The same may be said of the term 'certitude', which such writers have come to recognize as being a function of the intellect, and from which they have derived a number of inner aspects. According to them, the first stage is the knowledge of certainty, the second is the essence of certainty, while the third is the reality of certainty.

The thoughtful student should bear all of this in mind, and thus avoid being confused by variations in terminology.

It should be realized that there is a strong bond between the heart and the self—as there is also between the intellect and the self. They are closely bound one to another, like a hunting bow made of a combination of horn and wood whipped together. By virtue of their close proximity, each component benefits from the special properties of the other. It is actually the property of the horn to become pliable when heated; but the wood also bends with it when it bends and moves with its movement. Solidity and hardness are the characteristic qualities of the wood; and indeed the horn also acquires these properties. Now when an adjustment of the bow is required, and it is desired that this should be done in such a way as to maintain the balance which the form of the bow requires, then it is necessary that each of its characteristics should be attributed to its proper source, and that the extent of each modification should correspond to the strength of the original components. Another analogy of that bond might be quicksilver, in which the characteristics of a liquid and a metal are intimately combined.

Such then is the bond which gives rise to all the many mystical states. As soon as pure sobriety, unalloyed establishment and absolute permanency come into being, then all these visions disappear, and there remains neither ecstasy nor the ravings of the ecstatic. The Sufi is then indistinguishable from any normal person.

It should be borne in mind that the term 'stage' refers to an attribute which may be acquired by the seeker whilst on the path and which enables him to complete that journey. However the term has a far wider range than this and embraces a whole variety of conditions, circumstances and capacities. A stage arises in one individual in one form and in a different form in someone else. The term 'state' refers to the actual product of the stage: that is, the particular mode in which it appears to someone on one specific occasion and according to his particular capacity. Hence stage is regarded as an acquisition, while state is a gift. For example, the abandonment of the requirements of the carnal and aggressive selves is a stage; whereas the advantages arising from this—namely, serenity and purity and nobility of spirit—these are a state. Similarly, the impression which an exhortation may create in the mind of a seeker, and which may eventually bring him to the stage of repentance: this, too, is a state.

When it is in the fundamental nature of the self to require the satisfaction of its base desires, it is indispensable that it should be purified through repentance and renunciation. When its basic nature is irresolute and impetuous in the pursuit of its own requirements, then the necessary remedy is to place it in the power of the aggressive self, so that the individual may be stirred up against himself, and may begin to dislike himself and sit in judgment on himself. Many a time we have seen that a man begins to rebuke himself, take himself to task and express his regret and shame. This happens when the aggressive self dominates the carnal self. However, this effect cannot be achieved unless the point has been fully understood and has struck deep into the heart.

We have often observed that certain sayings impress the heart, and that the impression can last for a long time. This happens when the heart is ruled by the perceptive faculty. It is for this reason that the greatest Sufis have considered the rebuke to be the key to repentance.

It may happen that a person sees the world's vicissitudes and suddenly recoils from himself and desists from sin. Or it may be that he hears the sermon of a preacher at an opportune moment and his heart suddenly turns towards him. Or perhaps through association with men of God he may slowly become inclined to straightforwardness. Here the rebuke may be gradual rather than immediate, and it may give rise to passion.

The real nature of passion is to effect a change in the heart such that it is totally transformed and its hold over the bodily members is destroyed. Sometimes this passion may take the form of falling unconscious, sometimes of tearing one's clothes or making other involuntary movements. At times it appears as weeping and grieving, at times as a simple hatred of everything except reality and being drawn towards reality. By rebuke we mean the influx of the intellect into the heart. Passion is a function of the heart and the control which it exerts over the self. Afterwards wakefulness ensues, and that implies both vigilance and awareness.

It is thanks to the intellect that one is able to recognize disobedience for what it is, and hence to show anger and hatred towards it. The intellect proceeds according to the dictates of the heart and is constantly thinking of ways to meet its requirements. Consequently the individual is able to abandon disobedience, change his former ways, adhere to vows of obedience, starve his own self of its fraudulent machinations and obliterate its obstinacy. Thus the heart subjugates the bodily members, controls their habits and brings them under its own control and direction.

After this there comes abstinence from those pursuits which, though lawful, nonetheless hinder the work of the heart—whether the hindrance be an external one, such as a worldly occupation which takes up most of one's time and does not allow one to busy oneself with matters of ultimate importance; or else the hindrance may be a mental one, such as the love of property and people, since such love and affection are a hindrance to the sweet remembrance of God. Similarly, to spend one's time in conversation with people, or to engross oneself in poetry or intellectual matters are equally repugnant to the heart.

There then comes a phase of taking judicious stock of oneself moment by moment; that is, remaining constantly aware of one's state, to see whether one's time is passing in negligence and sin, or whether it is spent in acts of devotion. If the desired objective is being furthered, we should thank God for that, and think hard of ways to continue this trend and enhance it even. But if the reverse is the case, then we should repent anew. This, then, is what constitutes the purification of the self, regardless of whether it is accomplished at the outset or after the heart and the intellect have been purified. All of this is termed repentance.

The stage of repentance may have different forms. It is rather like when a young man attains maturity and the desire for the female sex makes its appearance in him: little by little the requirements of love, such as expending time and wealth and self in its pursuit, enter into his heart. So many varied indications of his love appear. In reality, however, love appears in man in one and the same form, and merely produces all these different conditions, which, in view of their common origin, the intellect considers as one. In the same way, when a man's carnal self is subjugated, and it accepts the control of the heart and intellect, so many different states appear, all of which the wise have subsumed under the name of repentance. Thus, the stage of repentance is one, but it bears many fruits and states.

In subjugating the self, the heart is assisted by four factors: eating little, sleeping little, speaking little and associating little with others. It is just as one would whip and goad a restive horse into submission.

One of the characteristics of the heart is to subjugate

the bodily members, modify their behaviour and use them to carry out particular tasks. The visible effect of this aspect of purification is called sincerity and propriety. Other effects are shame and embarrassment, confusion, penitence and contrition. The effect of this aspect of purification is called passion.

Another characteristic of the heart is to subjugate the carnal self and take no account of its frivolity and greed, and keep it willy-nilly under firm control. The effect of this aspect of the purification of the self is called patience.

A further characteristic of the heart is to conform with the intellect and to heed and accept its bidding. The effect of this aspect of purification is termed surrender to providence.

Yet another of its characteristics is loyalty to friends and close adherence to their customs. The effect of this aspect of purification is called piety and love of holy ritual.

One final characteristic is that, in comparison with the desired objective, everything else is found to be a simple matter; and because of its inclination towards the real, the heart suppresses any impulse to anger, avarice, love of dignity or extravagant hopes. The effect of this aspect of purification of the self is named magnanimity.

Thus we have seen that the fundamental stages of the heart are these: sincerity, passion, patience, reliance, surrender, piety, love of holy ritual, and magnanimity. This is the reason why the Sufis have spoken so much about these attainments and explained them so thoroughly.

Concerning the benefits which accrue from the purification of the intellect, as a result of its acquiescence in that which transcends it, these are twofold. The first is that a conviction concerning the supreme manifestation, which is established in the sacred fold of paradise, filters through to the individual from the sublime realms. A resolution forms in his mind, without his understanding exactly where it came from. He is certain about it in every detail; and yet he is unable to say a single word about it. 'The blind man knows he has a mother, but he has no idea what she looks like.' This kind of conviction needs to be completed by reliance and surrender; and it clothes both heart and self in a robe of its own colour.

A second benefit is this, that from the repositories of sublime knowledge, which in the Law are termed 'the tablet', and which in Sufi parlance are called 'the world of ideas', the mind is inundated with images of the future, either in dreams, or else in the waking state in the shape of visions and imaginings. This is known as revelation.

With regard to one's effectiveness in more mundane areas, there are two further benefits. First, the seeker's powers of conjecture and logical inference increase, and he may gain a true insight into the course of events. He may be able to see into the hearts of others and gain access to hidden information. Second, whatever happens to reach his ears from the Qur'an, the Traditions of the Prophet and from the sayings and doings of the ancients—all of this is, with God's grace, assimilated by his intellect; and he is thus able to understand perfectly the purpose behind every word and the interpretation of every tradition, as well as the associations and allusions implicit in every verse. The manifestation of the attributes and the names of God may illuminate his mind, rendering him for a moment both inwardly and outwardly submissive. Spiritual illuminations will appear to him in their most complete form. All of these are the fruits of purification and the benefits of training.

The corner-stone of purification is perpetual service. This is of equal value to each of the three faculties, and its benefits embrace all of their ramifications. At this point, however, there is a difference between earlier and later Sufis. The former used to ascribe more importance to the purification of the self, the intellect and the heart, together with their specific manifestations and peculiarities; and they placed most emphasis on the training of these three faculties, regarding perpetual service merely as the end-product and consummation of such training. The later Sufis, however, concerned themselves exclusively from the very outset with perpetual service.

They did not consider anything to be more important and useful than that. After completing and perfecting this relationship, they would then look to see what kind of shoot and leaf this seed had brought forth in the heart of the seeker, and what kind of flower this shoot would eventually produce. If by virtue of the soundness of nature and stability of temperament of the particular individual all the stages of attainment had been produced, well and good; if not, they proceeded to aim for what had not as yet appeared. In holding this view, the later Sufis were in fact on target. Doubtless this was a rare blessing which had been reserved for them.

Thus if certitude and love are gained before the purification of the self has occurred, then such a person is called 'the attracted' and 'the desired'. However, if purification of the self, repentance and the spiritual exercise occur before the appearance of conviction and the desire for love, then such a person is named 'the seeker' and 'the disciple'.

In general, perpetual service falls into two categories: type one is connected with the limbs and organs of the body and with the tongue. This entails spending one's life in prayer and reading the Qur'an with one's thoughts collected and one's heart in attendance. This is one of the fundamental principles of Sufism, and it has been explained exhaustively in such books as Abu Talib Makki's *Quwwat-ul-Qulub,* Al Ghazzali's 'Revival of Religious Sciences', Jilani's *Ghaniyat-ut-Talibin,* and Suhrawardi's 'Gifts of Deep Knowledge'.

The second type is connected with the heart and the intellect. Here the heart is occupied with the love of the Beloved and close attachment to the Beloved. The intellect is occupied with remembrance and awareness while breathing. In this connection we have not seen any path more profitable than that followed by the Masters of the Naqshbandi School. However, at this point there arises a difference of opinion.

Some people have been content to occupy themselves

with inner matters, and have not taken externals into account, regarding these as a simple affair. This is one of the errors of the later mystics. Concerning this matter, the substance of what the Masters of the Naqshbandi School have said is this: that it is sufficient to keep within the limits indicated by sublime tradition—not that one may deny the very foundations of the latter.

The whole point of engaging oneself in activities and exercises is that every faculty should be educated and that due consideration should be given to every stage.

The attainment of the stage of sincerity and the purification of the self and the bodily members are impossible without the outward display of devotion. When a man undertakes the obligation of perpetual service, and dedicates himself to it both inwardly and outwardly, never sparing himself even for a moment, and this quality penetrates his heart, intellect and self to the very core—deep, deep into his innermost depths—then inevitably every detail of the various stages will come into operation. In the science of behaviour, this quality serves as the substance, while the developmental stages are like forms. Once the wax has been made ready, then whatever image is desired can be fashioned from it. In the same way, the practice of perpetual service has first of all to be adjusted before each individual stage can be put right. 'First the throne is made firm; then it is decorated.'

When perpetual service has been duly adjusted, the appearance of the various stages will take place in accordance with the basic nature of the three human types outlined above. Thus the stage of sincerity will come easily to him whose heart by nature dominates both his bodily members and his behaviour and has brought them under control as a matter of course.

If the love of a particular community establishes itself in the heart of a man who is weak by nature, and yet his heart does not require him to follow the regulations of that community, and if its outward forms of behaviour, such as courteous speech, paying frequent visits and the giving of precious gifts do not alter his habitual ways—then such a person must be seen to have no hope whatsoever of completing the stage of sincerity.

There is another type of man who is not strong in his heart: when calamities assail him, he loses self-control and becomes impatient, fretful and distressed. Obviously such a man has no hope of perfecting the stage of patience and fulfilling its requirements.

Perpetual service is like a seed. The growth of a shoot with leaves and eventually a flower depends upon the fitness of the soil. So it has to be established whether the soil is by nature good or bad, since it is precisely upon that nature that the whole process will depend.

If perpetual service attains its perfect form without any of the stages revealing its splendour, then there is no harm in that. Sheikh Bayazid of Bistam has called such a person, who has practised perpetual service and yet not seen any vision, 'The King of those who remember God.'

Now that we have gained a general view, it is necessary to understand these developmental stages in detail, and briefly to discuss the method of studying them.

The meaning of sincerity is a correspondence between outward and inward. This refers to the truthfulness of states, not the truthfulness of words. It can come into existence only when the constitution of the heart is sound and the heart compels the body to move according to its instructions. There is a well known saying: 'When your heart submits, so also will your limbs.'

The heart rules over the bodily members, and by virtue of its love it modifies their patterns of behaviour. When this quality becomes innate in the heart and is maintained for a long time in close association with perpetual service, then a stage is created between these two attributes, and that stage is known as sincerity. As a result the disciple's body becomes submissive, and he begins to show courtesy and deference in his speech, and to treat all those who are associated with the Beloved as his own respected friends.

When, for example, he finds the name of God written on

a piece of paper, he reveres it, even though he has never been told to do so. Or if he hears someone pronounce the name of God, he at once says, 'May his glory be great!' and then lowers his gaze—even though he may never previously have seen this done by anyone else.

When perpetual service has been achieved, it is then necessary for the spiritual guide to propound the value of training the bodily members and looking after them carefully, so that through repeated practice, the heart should progress by way of obedience to a positive love of such training, until eventually the door is opened.

The term passion is used to describe the preoccupation of the heart with various states such as shame, grief, repentance, aversion for the world, etc.; and it is implicit in this notion that the bodily members are likewise controlled by such preoccupations. When through perpetual service both this capacity and that of sincerity are created in a man, and the spirits of the heart are somewhat reduced in stature, then the various states which ensue may be attributed to God. Because one's attention is turned towards God, and because of the diminished stature of the spirits of the heart, it becomes more difficult to ward off these states; and the bodily members become more passive. As a result fainting and other deranged actions are observed. This or that particular transport of passion represents a state; while the capacity for such transports, which is permanently fixed in the individual, represents a stage.

This stage is attained by eating less, remaining plunged in grief and awe, and turning one's back on finery, comfort and excitement. The rapture of passion is further facilitated by the avoidance of association with other people, especially those who deny the existence of such a state; or at very least one should feel ashamed for such people.

At this point, however, there is a widespread error, to which those who are unacquainted with passion fall prey. The mistake they make is this: even without the discipline of perpetual service, or the imbuing of the intellect with conviction, the human temperament is susceptible to delicious melodies and well-measured cadences, and is moved by them in precisely the same way that animals are. This phenomenon is then considered an important affair and counted as one of the stages of the saints. Not a bit of it: God forbid! What would be the attraction of a stage which is common to both man and the animals? But when the human temperament is wedded to perpetual service, it then remains to be seen whether the resultant offspring inclines more to the lower or the higher faculty.

Patience, too, also depends on firmness of heart and is born from the union between this firmness and perpetual service. It is attained in the same way as the other stages, namely, when the intellect gains control over the heart and supports it whenever a show of patience is required. In addition, one may bear in mind the reward reserved for the patient and the disgrace of the impetuous.

Trust is of two kinds. On the one hand there is reliance in the promise of God, which arises when divine inspiration or revelation filters through to the intellect from above, in such a way that there is no possibility of doubt. But then there is also a vice which resembles trust and which has commonly been confused with it. This vice manifests itself either in rashness and disregard for the consequences of one's acts, or else indulgence in luxury and neglecting all thought of livelihood for its sake.

Piety means abiding by the limits of Holy Law. Love for the signs of God means that one should love the Qur'an, the Prophet, the Kaaba—indeed everything relating to God, including his saints. Some people call this love 'annihilation in the Prophet' or 'annihilation in the spiritual guide'. Magnanimity and freedom signify that the heart is impervious to the impulses of the self, such as impetuosity, greed and impatience.

The later Sufis, particularly those of the Naqshbandi School, detected yet another state of the heart and brought it to perfection. The ancient mystics were not familiar with this type of state, even though on rare occasions and in a haphazard way something of that state also appeared in them. I am referring to the impression which is made on the mind of the disciple—the impression of a sublime objective.

To elaborate on this in greater detail, the minds of certain men have been invested with such a degree of aggressive and dominating energy, that whoever comes into their sphere of attention appears by contrast to be inferior and of small account, and is dominated and intimidated by them. If such a dominant individual comes into close contact with someone, then his own state of pleasure or grief invades that person. Men vary in their power of dominance: some possess it absolutely; some do not possess it at all; while there are others whose power of dominance lies somewhere in between.

This power generally appears when some such transaction as a discussion, an argument or a quarrel is taking place. The contagious effect of joy and grief is habitually associated with an interchange of some sort, or with some expression indicative of that emotional condition. Consequently people do not recognize this as being an independent faculty, separate from the rest; and thus they have no particular mental picture of its form and properties. When someone becomes engaged in perpetual service, and the various attributes of the heart, such as love, passion and longing, arise in him quite independently of anything said or done—nor is any need felt for such a connection—then this property of dominance, too, pervades all these attributes and takes up its allotted place among them. Then, when such a person imbued with this quality of dominance turns his attention to a pupil, and captivates his soul by virtue of his own aspiration, and views his pupil's heart and intellect in the light of that aspiration, he is able to pour whatever attribute he chooses, such as love or conviction, into his pupil's mind. This is called the 'impression of attention' and the 'look of acceptance'.

In fact the act of attention coupled with the power of dominance, which can infuse the student with one of the praiseworthy attributes, is a blessing of immense value.

An analogy would be when a man takes a flint and strikes a piece of iron on it to make sparks. Sometimes the spark flies and sometimes it does not; and if there is a spark, sometimes it falls to the ground and sometimes it lands in the tinder. However, there is another kind of man, who prepares a great fire, throwing all sorts of things into it, both fresh and dry, as and when he pleases, without taking into consideration the required conditions, and who thus tries to burn it all up indiscriminately. There is an immense difference between these two types.

When the seeker passes beyond the stage of certitude which is associated with words and prayer-exercises—beyond the stage of reverence for words and sounds—then it often happens that his perceptive and imaginative faculties begin to serve him. They fashion an image which has neither shape nor colour nor dimension, and provide conviction with an analogy by which to explain that image in detail. It is like the bond of affection by means of which the falcon, once released, may be brought back to its perch. In some minds, certitude simply elaborates itself into an imaginary form; this is known as a representational illumination, and can occur either in a waking or a sleeping state.

Revelation sometimes encounters an astonishing capacity to produce certain characteristic letters, movements, gestures and so on. These properties are sometimes of lasting effect and sometimes only characteristic of a certain stage. In order to acquire a detailed understanding of this subject, it is extremely useful to disengage oneself from brutish nature and fix one's attention on the inferior angels.

At this point popular mystics have fallen into a serious error, in that they have failed to understand the difference between subjective association and objective meaning.

Association may be understood in this way. When a mystic hears a verse from the Qur'an or a Tradition of the Prophet, his mind may switch to a form of knowledge which is other than the conventional meaning inferred by means of the commentary on the text and the allusions contained in it. In the case of an interior monologue, one thought attracts another, one thing recalls another. Such shifts of thought can occur both in sleep and the waking state. However, there are also other shifts, which may sometimes be interior monologue, sometimes the insinuations of the devil, and sometimes the promptings of the intellect. But in the case of the gnostic all of this may serve as a real inspiration and a true education.

Association is the product of the stage which the mystic has reached and the words which he hears. Doubtless you have experienced, when a professional story-teller is relating the story of Laila and Majnun, how the lover is reminded of his own tale of woe, and the times when his own beloved rejected or accepted his suit. As a result he is either delighted or highly disturbed. But this is not the story of Laila itself, nor is it to be inferred from it; rather it arises through the intimate association of the listener's developmental stage with the words he hears. The main point about association is the transference of understanding, not the particular modes of expression.

As you are probably aware, the Holy Prophet has dealt with the art of association in the course of his deliberations on the Qur'an, and has set in motion a vast river of knowledge concerning this. However, it is not the purpose of this book to discuss association, beyond briefly stating that it is an excellent and extensive science. The *Tafsir 'Ara'is* of al-Baqli, the *Haqa'iq* of Sullami, and many of the discourses of Ibn el-Arabi and Sheikh Suhrawardi relate to this subject.

When the seeker has completed the purification of the self, the heart and the intellect, and has gained the benefits accruing from this, the next requirement is the purification yet again of the self, this time in conjunction with the spirit and the secret faculty. The previous purification of the self was of a different type from that which is now required.

In further amplification of this point, the mischief perpetrated by the self is of two kinds. In the first instance the individual pursues his own requirements, whether these be the natural desires of his temperament or those of his aggressive self. Hence his intellect and his heart are disturbed, and much of his time is spent getting tainted by these vices. The remedy for this is that the intellect should control the heart and the heart should rule over the self; from the combination of these two forms of control, the various developmental stages should result.

In the second case the self has now forgotten its own requirements—its carnal and aggressive desires. Search as you may, you will no longer find in the self any image of a beloved, or any delight in sexual pleasures; and however much you investigate, you will not find in it any sign of love of dignity or greed for wealth. And yet a black pall of smoke rises up from the self, which blots out the face of both the spirit and the secret; a cloud of dust is stirred up which soils these two mirrors; a bitterness proceeds from the self which spoils the sweet taste of the spirit and the secret. No matter how diligently he may search for the origin of that dust-cloud, he cannot understand what it is; however much he applies his intellect, he is unable to work out where it came from. But the discerning gnostic is well-aware that all of this is the work of the self, whose viciousness never decreases even for a moment, and that nowhere is there any respite to be found from the struggle against it.

It should be remembered that the spirit has two essential attributes. First, it is attracted towards the supreme manifestation, which is established at the centre of the holy fold of paradise. The universal soul receives that illumination and unites with it. From there indescribable peace and tranquillity pour forth. The possession of this attribute is the highest stage of the spirit, and marks the end-point of its movement back to its original abode.

Second, the spirit may be attracted towards other pure spirits and towards the exalted assembly, and may be united with them. This attribute receives their impression, just as wax receives the impression of the signet ring when it is pressed into it, and the engravings of the ring are stamped on the wax. In fact this impression is a generalized one, which accommodates itself to a whole variety of specific impressions according to the requirements of situations and circumstances. Sometimes it may take the form of a speech; in which case the intellect is uppermost; at other times it might be an event, indicating that the heart is predominant. This attribute constitutes the lowest rank of the spirit, in that it falls short of its own sublime levels, owing to the adherence to it of certain innate impurities.

On certain occasions it has been personally experienced that a light issuing from the supreme manifestation is shed upon the spirit, which by way of a simile might be compared to sunlight without the presence of any sun.

In short this attraction, which may be either towards the supreme manifestation or towards the exalted assembly, is the expression of a special love. This differs, however, from the love of faith which develops when the intellect becomes convinced of the true doctrines. It also differs from the longing and ardour which arises when the heart is infused with one of the states of passion; for those are states of disquietude and agitation.

Special love is like the inclination of the earth towards its centre, or the inclination of air towards its place of rest. The wise understand that this inclination is one thing which has appeared in two forms. At the time of separation, it appears as longing and restlessness; while at the time of the envisioned union, it appears in the form of peace and repose. Thus, special love is this inclination itself, and by extension it is the desired peace and repose. What causes it is the attraction which the supreme manifestation exerts on human spirits, and by virtue of which the latter are naturally drawn towards the former. An analogy of such active and passive attraction might be the relationship between a magnet and a piece of iron. This, then, is special love: to cleave to the supreme manifestation and hold it in a tight embrace, until one is consumed in the flames of intimacy. And this is the hidden sense (and God knows best) of the quatrain:

> A bulbul with a pretty petal in its bill
> was piping many a melancholy trill.
> Said I: 'At the height of union, why such woe?'
> —'Tis the Loved One's glory keeps us busied so.'

Similarly, the secret faculty also has two essential attributes. Of these the first is to contemplate the supreme manifestation, to comprehend it, to be present before it and to gain knowledge of it. This is the highest stage of the secret.

The second is to meet and contemplate the pure spirits and the exalted assembly, which gather round the supreme manifestation and are attracted towards it. But this attribute is the lowest rank of the secret, in that it falls short of its higher levels, owing to the adherence of certain natural impurities. Its characteristic effect is to give information about the supreme manifestation, to become aware of it and be able to distinguish it from what is other than it. But it does not receive an impression, like the wax and the ring. Hence if the intellect is foremost, there will be a revelation; and if the heart lends its support, there will be deep knowledge.

There is a difference between the contemplation experienced by the secret and the certitude which flows into the intellect. The difference is that contemplation takes place in the presence of the thing sought, while certitude means believing in things absent and acknowledging the unseen.

At this point a serious error often occurs; and it is not within the capacity of every ecstatic to resolve it. At times the imagination serves the intellect, and for the sake of certitude it fashions an explanation and pictures an imaginary form. Now if this imaginary form comes to dominate the mind of the ecstatic, he may conclude that this is contemplation. Then, however much he brings his scientific and mystical knowledge to bear on the problem of distinguishing the two, he will make no progress. The reason for this is that, although it may be said that contemplation is a gratuitous state and that the imaginary form is an induced state, this does not cover the case; because if induced states are produced for a long time, they begin to resemble gratuitous ones; and, conversely, in the beginning gratuitous states may be confused with induced ones.

It may be objected that the imagination is restricted in its scope, even if that scope is extremely subtle; whereas the supreme manifestation is not subject to any limitations whatsoever. But that does not help matters either, since the imaginary form, by virtue of its extreme subtlety and delicacy, may be confused with something purely incorporeal, and it is impossible for the mystic to make a distinction. Again it may be objected that the imaginary form exists only in the senses, while contemplation takes place outside of the senses—indeed outside of space altogether. But what is the point of that, if in fact one is unable to distinguish between what is encompassed by the senses and what lies outside of them?

In short, this is an extremely difficult problem, which can only be solved by someone who has perfected the stage of establishment. And yet, even if this imaginary form were to be mistaken, by reason of its delicacy, for the purely incorporeal, it would still be a wonderful alchemy which brought one nearly to the stage of the secret.

Between them, the spirit and the secret are the basis of many wonderful states. If both of them reach their original abode and ascend towards the height of their progress, and if the self meanwhile desists from its mischief, then contemplation of the supreme manifestation will be achieved, accompanied by a wondrous attraction, a rare intimacy, and an extraordinary all-consuming love. This state is usually called 'close union'.

If the heart and intellect become infused with this state, then both sensory and bodily functions cease. This form of close union is termed 'absence' or 'non-existence'.

If the secret falls short of some of its functions as it moves to the height of its progress, then a state will appear which is named 'descent'. This is comparable to the state of the nightingale, which, when in the presence of the flower, becomes so immersed in contemplation that it pays no attention to the flower. If the secret is even less in evidence, then a state will emerge which is called 'intimacy'. If the secret is engaged in its own function and the spirit remains in general abeyance, then a state will arise which is called 'deep knowledge'; but if the spirit is even less in evidence, then a state appears which is termed 'discrimination', but in this case the subject does not attain to the delights of contemplation.

If the smoke of the self rises up in this state and mingles with these two faithful friends, spirit and secret, and disturbs their functions, then the resultant state is called 'contraction'. However, if the self acquiesces in this state, derives pleasure from it, and delights in singing the praises of that intimacy, then such a state is known as 'dilation'.

If on certain occasions close union is achieved and on others it is not, then that state is termed 'manifestation and concealment'. If it appears for a moment in a fragmentary form and is then effaced, this state is known as 'glimpses and flashes'. All this happens in the early phases of progress from the stages of the heart and the intellect towards those of the secret and the spirit.

Sometimes close union is concealed by some of the veils of the airy soul. However, remnants of it may appear in the form of utterances, happenings, thoughts and the promptings of truth. If the heart is dominant then these subtle effects resemble a mystical state; and the knowledge which emerges from them does so by means of the heart. If the intellect is foremost, then such effects have more in common with perception and intelligence; and the state which enters the mind from these subtleties does so by means of the intellect.

If the spirit and the secret come down to their lowest

level, they will be attached to the exalted assembly and have access to it. However, if such attachment and access are concealed by veils of the airy soul, then they will make their appearance in the form of utterances, thoughts and angelic impulses.

It sometimes happens that the secret is at its most highly developed stage, while the spirit is at the lowest stage; at other times the reverse is the case. Every situation has its own particular characteristics, which only an expert can comprehend. 'There is a time for every word, and a place for every subtle point.'

It should be understood that although the Sufis have spoken much about annihilation and permanency, they have not made the matter entirely clear. What the present writer has been able to discover on this point is this: within their own limits, each of the bodily limbs and organs, and each of the faculties possesses its own separate jurisdiction. When they all come together in a single entity, then one of two situations is bound to ensue. Either there will be such an intimate mingling, blending and bonding among them as is found in quicksilver, in which the properties of metal and liquid are combined— or such as is found in the bonding of horn and wood to make a bow. Alternatively, each one of them may remain independent in its own sphere of influence and simply afford the other faculties such support as is in keeping with the constitutional requirements of the body.

In the case of the first alternative the states obtained will be possession, inebriation, absorption and passion; while in the second case sobriety, establishment and constancy are produced. The greatest of men is he who has attained establishment, and whose every faculty is independently in its own state.

In the situation where all the faculties are mixed together, if the bodily members and the carnal and aggressive selves take control, then such a person will become one of the sinners and hypocrites mentioned in the previous chapter. But if perpetual service has had an effect upon the heart, and the heart thus affected gains mastery over the intellect, the bodily members and the self, then possession, inebriation and passion will ensue.

It has often been observed that the intellect of the man of heart is overwhelmed, with the result that in such moments of upheaval he does not understand anything either of this world or the next. He does not even perceive his own best interest, and is oblivious to heat, cold and pain. Occasionally he may throw himself down on the ground—sometimes even from a height. Such things are frequently seen in the people of passion. However, if the intellect prevails, constancy and persistence in knowledge are achieved.

The first situation may be termed annihilation, and the second one permanency; or the first is possession and the second establishment; or the first is called inebriation and the second one sobriety.

When the spirit prevails over the heart, the bodily members and the self, then the ensuing state is known as absorption. But when the secret faculty prevails over them, the resultant state is called absence.

The foregoing is a description of the annihilation of base existence and the permanent survival of spiritual existence. Subsequently there is yet another annihilation, which will be described in the next chapter.

In brief, the method of purifying all these faculties is perpetual service. One should devote oneself both inwardly and outwardly to remembrance, so that every level should receive its due share. The process is analogous to pouring water on the hidden roots of a tree, so that branches and leaves will grow and flowers and fruit will appear according to a fixed pattern, in keeping with the nature of the tree.

To go into detail: vocal prayer, beating one's breast, breath control, the secret lesson, which is a legacy of the Masters of the Naqshbandi School, the contemplation of music and designs—all of these excite longing in the soul and bring it to life. The observance of purity at all times, the serene light of Quranic recitation, mystical exercises, and the cultivation of the Uwaisi relationship with the souls of the saints[4]—all of these provide nourishment for the soul. In the same way, contemplating the attributes of God and meditating on his names will bring the intellect to the seat of splendour. Pure remembrance, i.e., soundlessly and wordlessly remembering God, a Naqshbandi practice, will awaken the secret faculty.

It has repeatedly been observed that the self is forever craving the satisfaction of its base desires for such things as sensuality or superiority and dominance over one's peers. However, at times the individual restrains his self and opposes it, with the result that a fierce conflict arises within him. At the time a great deal of bitterness is experienced; but when the dust settles and the agitation ceases, a wonderful light descends from the spirit and envelops the seeker both inwardly and outwardly. This is a rare alchemy, with which most people are not acquainted—a magnificent fortune, to which no stranger ever found his way. Shaikh Ibrahim Adham was alluding to this same light and sweetness when he said that he had twice seen his self reach its desired goal, and he related two stories about conflict.[5]

According to us, the purification of the faculties is recognized in a number of ways. First, the seeker will find sweetness in the quality which we have specified for each faculty: he is contented with it and takes pleasure in it. Second, a particular relationship arises within each person according to his developmental stage. Thus, the man of certainty is the man of intellect; while the man of passion and longing is the man of heart. Someone who is connected via remembrance is the man of the secret faculty; and the person connected through the Uwaisi relationship is the man of spirit. Finally, the individual witnesses various happenings which demonstrate the purification of these faculties.

It should be understood that, when the seeker has suf-

[4] See footnote p. 4.
[5] See Attar's *Tadhkaratul-Auliya* and Hujwiri's 'Revelation of the Veiled'.

ficiently perfected his faculties, that faculty will finally predominate which was originally strong by nature. Thus a seeker whose heart is strong will persist in his passion, longing and disquietude, even though he has perfected all his other faculties. The man of intellect will always delight in thought-associations and spiritual illuminations, even though he may be fully acquainted with all the other faculties. Concerning this there are many profound remarks in the discourses of Ibn el-Arabi. Similarly the man of spirit will relish all that is pertinent to the spirit; while the man of the secret will take pleasure in the influences of the secret faculty '... each party rejoicing in what is theirs.'[6]

A word of warning: if some of the adept's initial behaviour appears strange, there is no cause for offence. The explanation is simply that he is allowing himself to be ruled by his dominant faculty.

There now follow two further extremely subtle points. First, the constitution of a number of people travelling on the path is such that their heart is usually locked inextricably in the fetters of the carnal self. When such people eventually manage to free themselves from the coarse veils of the self, then inevitably the requirements of their carnal self will be extremely subtle and delicate. Thus they may be dominated by the desire to look at adolescent youths or to listen to flute music. Such pleasures tend to attract their heart and intellect. And yet this combination of baseness together with perpetual service produces such wonderful results, that ordinary people are totally baffled. It was in this connection that certain of our predecessors said to some people: 'For God's sake, just do it and move on!' And it is to this situation, too, that the following line refers: 'The blasphemy of a perfect man is tantamount to faith.' It is in this light that one should judge the wild behaviour which is recorded of certain perfected men. You have probably read a good deal about such matters in the accounts of the later Sufis.

The second point is this: during the initial period of

[6] Qur'an 30.32.

Islam the bodily faculty was dominant; that is to say the heart faculty was totally engrossed in organizing the energies of the body. What was said by the mystics of this epoch accords with the outward form of the Law, even though certain specially gifted individuals among them had come to a general understanding of the hidden faculties.

In these pages we have presented the fundamentals of the entire science of Junaid, Lord of the Sufi Tribe. And God knows best.

Chapter Six

THE HIDDEN FACULTIES

The purification of the hidden faculties is accomplished through the sciences of symbolism and ultimate realities. Before launching into an enquiry concerning the hidden faculties, it should be understood that the real nature and the effects of these faculties are unfamiliar to most minds, and that most people do not benefit from being told of them. In fact there are only two types of person who stand to gain by hearing of these things. The first is someone who has already come close to developing them completely, and who has acquired the capacity to purify them. If such a person turns his attention to this present investigation, the conception he forms of these things will be the correct one, and it will open the door to success. The second type is someone who has been blessed with a general knowledge of these hidden faculties, but lacks the capacity to understand them in detail. If such a person reads this present investigation, his general knowledge will be transformed into a detailed one, and his acquired learning will combine with that which is God-given, and the two will become as one.

May God have mercy on whomsoever, when he encounters an obscure word in these investigations, either understands and accepts it, or else refers it to its author, so that the latter may produce an explanation of these sciences on that Day when every man will present his secrets before the Lord; thus, what is right and what is wrong will be made manifest to everyone.

Briefly, when the seeker has dealt with the five faculties which have already been mentioned, he then has to concern himself with the sublime spirit. The sublime spirit is composed of two parts.

One part is known as the rational soul. This is a bubble in the ocean of the universal soul, or an image formed from its wax, or it is an individual within the universal, or it is in some way a part of reality; each of these analogies can be applied to it. Every soul, whether it be mineral or vegetable or animal or angelic or satanic, is a bubble or a miniature image of that universal soul. Every soul, however, has its own sphere of influence. The perfected souls are the final cycle of souls, while the heavenly souls constitute the first cycle. Thus, just as in one sense the heavenly souls are nearest to the universal soul, in another sense the perfected souls are also the nearest to it; however there is a vast gulf between the one type of nearness and the other.

If you wish to understand this question more clearly, then you should realize that every soul has its own particular substance, and that the universal soul is manifested according to the capacity of that substance. Thus, for each separate substance the universal soul appeared dressed in a particular raiment. Once a substance became purified by the grace of the universal soul, it was able to receive a soul of its own. In the same way, when through fresh enhancement it became further purified, it inevitably became fit to receive a soul which was subtler, purer and more intelligent than the first.

When the elements assembled and combined with one another, and the physical world came into existence, then the ocean of the universal soul was stirred into agitation, and clothed itself in the finest forms of the physical world. The texture of that garment was entirely dependent on the constitution of that world. Then a fresh enhancement appeared, the function of which was to extract various of the component properties of the elements, to lend these properties the support of its abundance of form, and to assemble all these tiny component parts under a single bountiful command. This new enhancement became known as the mineral soul.

When mineral souls appeared in the world in all their profusion, and many of the elemental compounds were illuminated by their light, the universal soul was again stirred into agitation within the most refined and rarefied and most nearly incorporeal of the minerals, and appeared clad in a special form which depended for the fabric of its existence on the mineral form. The function of this fresh enhancement was to absorb the elements in the mineral body, and with them to clothe itself in a suitable garment, and regulate its nutrition and growth according to the measure allotted to it in the framework of the universal expediency.

When the vegetable souls multiplied, and the elemental combinations became illuminated by this light, the universal soul was stirred into agitation yet again. Clothed in a particular form, it pervaded the finest of the vegetable organisms. The effect of this was to produce the voluntary sensation and movement which characterize the animal soul.

After this grace had penetrated deep into physical matter and had organized the world according to this scheme, the universal soul rose once more into agitation; and assuming yet another form, it appeared transfigured in the finest animal organisms. The result of this transfiguration was the appearance of the intellect, the heart and the self, together with the properties peculiar to each of them. This topic has already been discussed in a previous chapter.

Once more, when this grace had illuminated the world, the universal soul was stirred into renewed agitation. It clothed itself in a particular form and appeared in all its splendour in the finest of human beings. The effect of this effulgence was the appearance within an individual selfhood of the impulses of the universal soul, which is the administrator of all that exists in the universe, and the influx into this bubble and likeness of knowledge and spiritual attainments.

Thus the gradations of these fundamental essences are

in fact due to each new enhancement which descended from the universal soul. Their classification corresponds to the way in which matter was originally organized. But when the language of the learned failed to explain this gradation and classification, they fell back on an arbitrary system which was a mere semblance of the real one, and reported on that instead.

The perfect man is, in our view, just as much a separate species among the various kinds of men, as man is a separate species within his own genus. Just as man is deemed superior to the animals by virtue of his universal outlook, so too the perfect man is superior to other men by virtue of the systematic refinement of his five faculties, which took place when the universal soul made its appearance in his particular selfhood and made the latter an appendage of its will. There are many such qualities in the perfect man, and to give a full account of them all would take too long. Briefly, the perfect man is the nearest of all individual souls to the universal soul. The difference in degree of proximity depends on the individual's capacity to receive the abundant grace which is poured down on it from the universal soul.

The second part of the sublime spirit is known as the celestial spirit. This, too, is a bubble in the ocean of the universal soul. But after the universal soul was stirred into agitation, it brought into existence a world which was an offshoot of that of the heavenly souls and which is known as the world of ideas. Initially a bubble of the universal human form appeared; and after a long period had elapsed that one form became fragmented into a great many forms.

The truth about the human form is that in its essence it is not universal: rather it is an individual represented in the substance of the world of ideas. However, that individual is formed in such a way that it matches whoever is placed in front of it. From this point of view we may call it universal man.

These myriad human forms, because of their own

specific properties, are attracted towards the supreme manifestation residing at the heart of the universal soul. The reason for this attraction is that, compared to all the other souls in the three kingdoms of nature, human souls are closest to the universal soul.

To sum up, there are two parts to the sublime spirit, and both are blended and mixed together. One part constitutes its substance and the other its form. The rational soul, which is a bubble that has come to the surface of souls in the physical world, is of the nature of substance; while the celestial spirit, which is likewise a bubble on the surface of the world of ideas, partakes of the nature of form.

It is in this way that a sculptor may form an image in his mind and beyond that image there is revealed a real image, existing an absolutely independent existence. It is neither conceptual nor external, but has an existence which it is beyond the scope of the framework laid down by the universal expediency to eliminate, and which is firmly rooted in the universal soul itself. Then the sculptor simply models his material from one shape to another, until he has made it correspond with the image imprinted in his mind. In the same manner, God in his absolute wisdom transforms souls from one state to another, until the rational soul has achieved a condition that corresponds with the ideal form, which appeared long before the rational soul first came into existence. God's law has always taken this course, that it is wiser to reveal form and conceal substance. 'The beloved's love is completely concealed, while that of the lover is proclaimed by two hundred drums and trumpets.'

The first journey of the gnostic is to the supreme manifestation; while his final journey is to absolute selfhood.

At the very heart of this sublime spirit an extremely bright point has been placed. It is as it were a soul of this soul; and this soul is like a body for it. That shining point is named the pure intellect. It would be outside the scope of this treatise to give a detailed account of it; however, we might say this much: that the Pure Essence, God, has left a sample of itself. Alternatively we could say that it is a characteristic of the Pure Essence that at one stage it is entirely engrossed in self-contemplation, while at other stages, despite its purity, it descends; however, in the course of that descent it loses none of its purity—unlike other things the purity of which is opposed to such a descent. Or else we could say that when the gnostic turns his gaze upon himself, and plunges deep into contemplation of the ultimate source of his arising, then the utmost limit of his vision is that essential shining point. He imagines that this point is in the middle of his own spirit; whereas in fact it dwells, in its unalloyed simplicity, in an illustrious abode. How is it possible for man, this handful of dust, to think of that most rare and treasured being as his guest? But because his vision has penetrated to the reality of realities, it appears to him as if this point existed in the very centre of his spirit.

At this point three possible interpretations emerge. The first is more disciplined and is advocated by the man whose pure intellect is enveloped in the veil of his sublime spirit and inherently bound up with it. Such bonding is analogous to that of metal and liquid in quicksilver. Thus, when this man turns to ecstasy, he finds in the ensuing revelations a sample of the essence and a legacy from the primal being which are more appropriate to him.

The second is closer to intoxication. Its proponent is the type of man whose pure intellect is by nature separated from the veil of the spirit, and whose subtle faculties are all annihilated in that pure intellect.

The third possibility is associated rather with pure sobriety of mind, complete establishment and absolute permanence. Its advocate is someone in whom one faculty does not dominate another. 'Oh God, show us the realities of things as they really are!'[1]—is the language appropriate to this state.

[1] Attributed to the Prophet Muhammad.

In short, these differences in interpretation have arisen out of differences in capacity among individual seekers. This is a point which should constantly be borne in mind when considering the great variations among them. And God knows best.

Likewise, when Lord Jesus saw these three parts and perceived their origin in all its glory and simplicity, he proceeded to establish the evangelical knowledge of the three persons of the trinity. To one of these he gave the name 'Father', and that is the central core of the essence of God. The second he called the 'Son', and that is the universal soul. The third one he called the 'Holy Spirit', and that is the supreme manifestation, which is established in the heart of the heavenly fold. However, the Christians totally failed to understand what is an extremely obscure topic: all they managed to produce was error and deviation. They were left behind, like a donkey stuck in the mud.

The Glorious Qur'an rejected their error, and demonstrated the meaning of obedience.[1] Glory be to God! The bold-hearted hear so many obscure subtleties uttered by the tongues of Truth; yet they know how to place every point where it belongs. But what an ignorant band of fools that was, who, when one obscure point issued from the presence of the spirit of God, became confounded and gave up without finding the right way. As the Arab poet says:

> Glass after glass
> of the drink of love:
> so how does wine taste, then,
> and how does it look?

However, this is a vast subject and lies outside our present discussion.

When these three sources have been clearly understood, it should also be plain that the influences of the hidden faculties, i.e., the concealed, the sacred light, the

---

[1] i.e., that Jesus is the *servant* of God.

deeply concealed and the ego, are all derived from these three sources.

When the gnostic's journey passes beyond minor sainthood, which has already been explained in our discussion of the path of Junaid, then one of two states will inevitably ensue.

The first alternative is that the influence of the celestial spirit is dominant, in which case the gnostic is attracted towards the supreme manifestation and attains a wonderfully close communion with it. While this communion is actually taking place, his pure intellect joins with the supreme manifestation; after which he starts on an indescribable ascent towards the Pure Essence, from which he receives something which cannot be interpreted. If it is called a contemplative vision, it is not really that; if it is called union, it cannot be said to partake of the nature of union either. It is simply a forgotten dream. However, this much we do know: it really is something, but it cannot be explained. This path is named the path of the prophetic inheritance.

The second alternative is that the influence of the rational soul is dominant; and this bubble loses itself in the ocean of the universal soul. The mark of this bubble's obliteration is seen in the welling up in the soul of the universal influence. This characteristic can have an overall effect, though sometimes it is only knowledge that is affected, in which case the gnostic's view culminates in absolute reality, in which every particular is established. But sometimes certain universal influences are also transmitted, with the result that one of the following states arises. Either the individual may see himself as the primary objective, with absolute reality included within himself as the secondary objective; or else he may perceive absolute reality as the primary objective, with himself and the whole world established within it—just as contingent existence stands within essence, or just as organic manifestations stand in external existence, from which they arise; or just as the accidental forms, which come in and out of existence, stand in matter. A third possibility is that the vision of the rational soul is completely diverted from its own existence, and nothing remains except absolute reality. This in turn gives rise to two further possibilities.

Either the absolute selfhood may replace the individual selfhood, and the gnostic may regard the individual selfhood as being the absolute selfhood; or else he may become oblivious of the individual selfhood, neither confirming it nor denying it nor interfering with it. He neither replaces it with the absolute selfhood, nor does he remember it as a separate entity. In Sufi parlance this is called illumination of the essence. Here the ultimate vision of the gnostic is the universal soul. From there he ascends towards the Pure Essence and gains something from it but does not know how to interpret it, or how to explain that forgotten dream, or how to conceive that which lies so far beyond. This path is named the major sainthood. However, whatever the path may be, prophetic inheritance or major sainthood, it makes little difference.

The sublime spirit envelopes the pure intellect in the same way as a piece of cotton is wrapped round a precious pearl; and the purity and fineness of that pearl is not seen save behind that veil. The influence of the sublime spirit is dominant, whether or not the influence of the heavenly spirit or of the rational soul, or both of them, is also present; and the influence of the pure intellect is likewise overruled by it and concealed under its veil. It is for this reason that perception of the Pure Essence produces nothing but bewilderment, and nothing can be said of it except that it is a forgotten dream. Whoever attains to this level, whether he arrived by this path or that path or both paths, '... is most perfect, most magnificent in rank and most illustrious in degree.'

It frequently happens that the pure intellect declares its independence, stirs within itself and rises up in agitation. Somehow it tears down the veil, so that its purity and fineness come into view. Thereupon all these subtle faculties are somehow annihilated, and only the pure intellect remains. The person who has achieved this stage is spoken of in one of two ways: either from the viewpoint of the supreme manifestation or from the viewpoint of the universal soul. He is able to distinguish one from the other; but in point of fact both of them are beyond his understanding. It is as if a conversation were percolating through to him from above: an inspiration is reaching him; an impulse is pouring down on him.

From the foregoing you will have understood, among other things, that the reality of man is vastly increased by the diversity of these relationships. The subtle faculties form into subdivisions, each of which is given a name. Thus, the combination of the sublime spirit with a dominant celestial spirit and a quiescent pure intellect requires a particular name of its own; and the name given is 'sacred light'. The combination of the sublime spirit with a dominant rational soul and a quiescent pure intellect also requires a name of its own, and is thus referred to as the 'concealed' faculty. When the pure intellect appears and subjugates both these spirits and assimilates their properties, then this, too, requires a name, and that name is the 'deeply concealed' faculty. This concludes our review of these most excellent qualities. And God knows best.

Some people experience yet another state which the intellect is unable to comprehend. The intellect has an area within which it may roam about and exert itself; but beyond that area it cannot pass, and it has no idea of the conditions obtaining outside. Of course, the intellect does not see the situation like this; in fact it emphatically denies that it is so—God forbid! But now that step by step our discussion is approaching such obscure truths, it is appropriate to make some remarks about this state as well. 'Once the water is over a man's head, one fathom or ten makes little difference.'

The perfection of the gnostic rises above the pure intellect: a stage is reached when the universal soul takes the place of his body and the Pure Essence becomes his soul.

Then, by dint of the science of presence, he sees the whole universe within himself. Now the science of presence is fundamentally rooted in the Pure Essence; so he regards this particular selfhood as being distinct from the other forms of selfhood. Or perhaps it may be that he is simply oblivious of it; in which case it does not seem to him that knowledge or inspiration percolate down to him from above: instead he sees the upheavals of fate and the inner ferment of knowledge and inspiration as having arisen from within himself, with one intuition giving rise to another, and one thought causing depression while another gives rise to pleasure. This state is called the 'illumination of the essence'; and it is impossible to render it full justice either in this world or the next.

However, a hint of that state does appear, and time after time something is manifested from behind the veil. God willing, it will appear more clearly when the elemental garb is cast aside. 'The veil of my soul's face is covered in dust: happy the day when I throw off that veil!'

It is an exquisite state. We know that it is beyond our powers to do justice to this stage of development. We know, too, that we have encompassed it and reached its summit; but nevertheless the intellect is at a loss to explain it, and as for expressing it in words, the tongue is dumbstruck. It is quite different from the state of agitation and ferment of the pure intellect which was described before. That was all a shadow, and this is the original reality; that was all words, and this is action. That was all hearsay, and this is the one who knows.

The annihilation of spiritual existence and the permanency of the Divinity are terms which refer to the power which the Real exerts over created being, and the power which the concealed faculty exerts over all the other faculties—or simply over the faculty of the sacred light together with the pure intellect. A special connection arises between the major selfhood and the other faculties, including the hidden faculties. This power can be of two types: power of actions, and power of the Essence.

The power of actions is seen when a trace of the absolute selfhood percolates down to the individual selfhood. A dewdrop of absolute being may penetrate a particular being through the channels of the subtle faculties. Influences from the absolute world pour down into the world of particularization, by way of analogy and imitation. It could be compared to the way in which black bile is associated with earth, yellow bile with fire, and phlegm with water. Similarly there are certain faculties in the reality of man which take after devils, angels, beasts, or plant life. Likewise, certain knowledge and states are found in the individual selfhood, which may be regarded as mimicking those of the absolute selfhood. It is from there that they are inherited, and to this that they are attached.

One of the greatest of all capacities is to be able to see the universe in the Real and the Real in the universe; or to close one's eyes and forget the universe in one's contemplation of the Real; or in some such way to discover the universal order. The first two states cannot be realized until both capacities are combined. If there were only the capacity for absolute being, then the characteristics of the universe could not be witnessed; and if there were only the capacity for individual being, then absolute reality could not be observed. The one combines with the other, and together they produce wonders. The ecstatic transports of the Sufis, such as incarnation and union, are the result of this mixture. But once the seeker has seen the Real within the Real, he has no more to do with such fantasies.

There is a state far superior to this, in which a divine impulse is transmitted, either from the supreme manifestation, or from the universal soul, or from a place where there is no differentiation whatsoever into supreme manifestation and universal soul—a place where all is oneness in oneness, simplicity in simplicity. This divine impulse, then, pours down from one of these sublime regions, becomes suspended with the individual selfhood and mingles with the substance of this bubble. Subsequently this person becomes like a limb in relation to the universal expediency and the major administration.

A state is created in the intellect, self and heart of this person which originally is one of the spiritual states, but which is more akin to the states of the exalted assembly. Eventually, in keeping with the requirements of the universal administration, the attention of human minds is turned towards this person. An effect corresponding to the power of the supreme manifestation, which is present in the heart of the greater body, is transmitted by this person to the people. Such a person is called perfect. His effect takes the form either of a new religious dispensation, or a new science, or the foundation of one of the mystical orders, or the removal of tyranny, or a change in the customs and habits of the people. The bringer of a new dispensation would be a great prophet; while the remover of tyranny would be the deputy of God.

Here there arises a great ambiguity, which can only be resolved by those who have achieved absolute establishment. The ambiguity is this: that sometimes the divine impulse does not come down from the sublime regions; what occasionally happens instead is that the impulse is represented in the world of ideas in the likeness of a mighty form, and then descends into the minds of certain human beings. It is not possible to distinguish between the impulse which arises out of the sublime regions expressly for one particular individual, and the impulse which arises out of the world of ideas for whomsoever should chance to receive it. Thus one situation can be mistaken for the other. A further complication arises from the fact that when an impulse from the sublime regions is directed towards one particular perfect man, every limb and organ of the greater body is filled with that impulse, by order of the universal expediency. As a result of this a wide avenue is opened up from the world of ideas to the intellect and heart of this perfect individual. This circumstance has doubled the possibility of confusion and made discrimination even more difficult.

The power of the Essence is not itself susceptible to description. In trying to comprehend such matters the intellect gains nothing but disappointment. However, what little can be said is this: just as the pure intellect is a secret which is derived from the Essence, and this derivation is a matter which is known as to its reality but unknown as to its quality, in the same way a secret is derived from the pure intellect which is known as to its reality but unknown as to its quality. This secret encompasses all the faculties, both manifest and hidden, and it influences and controls them all, even the bodily organs and limbs, and in some way makes them implicitly follow its lead and tinges them with its own colouring.

The faculties, then, are derived by means of this secret from the pure intellect, and the pure intellect itself has a special relationship with the major selfhood. An analogy for this relationship might be the sun shining upon some glasses of varying shape, size and colour. All these glasses produce a wonderful lustre, and light streams continuously from them. Or else it is like a ruby set in the middle of a piece of crystal, permeating the whole with its colour.

If you examine the reality of this situation closely, it is apparent that the power of actions and that of the Essence are basically the same. The difference lies in the amount of power present. When there is little of it present, it is impossible to recognize its effects apart from those of the world; and when there is more power, its effects appear without any admixture. God knows best.

To sum up, there is no point in saying more than this. All in all we should be better advised to step back from this abyss, and return to discussing certain essential points concerning the subtle faculties.

> The pen melted,
> chameleon-like,
> in the hand of thought:
> the ink ran dry before the sketch
> could become your true likeness.

It should be understood that whereas the actions of the bodily limbs and organs are manifest, clear and perceptible, the states of the self, heart, spirit and secret are latent and concealed. The former belong to the visible world and the latter to the invisible. By the same argument, whatever proceeds from the visible faculties is manifest and clear, and whatever proceeds from the invisible faculties is latent and concealed and cannot be comprehended either intellectually or emotionally. For this purpose there is another extremely subtle and delicate sensory faculty, which in Sufi parlance is called 'taste'.

At this point a great many people fall into error: since they are familiar with what can be comprehended by intellect and emotion, they do not relish the thought of something which is comprehended by means of a finer sense. It may even be that they can in fact comprehend it, and yet they still deny comprehension of it. The reason for this is that the aspirations of the majority have sunk to such an extremely low level, that they can only recognize the pleasures of the senses. If ever there is anything that is not apparent to the external senses, they deny its existence.

The remedy for this spiritual malady is, first, to find out about this sensory faculty and to recognize the scope and quality of this type of comprehension. After that habitual attachment to familiar things should be broken off, and one should cultivate the habit of acquiring this subtle form of comprehension. The intuitive sense is an imaginative power, not one of the outward senses; the characteristic of this form of comprehension is that it is devoid of any connection with form and dimension.

The perception of incorporeal things belongs exclusively to the rational soul, not to comprehension, imagination and fantasy. What characterizes the rational soul is that it is completely free of material attributes.

It should also be understood that the purification of the

sublime spirit would be quite unthinkable without the seeker's turning his attention to the supreme manifestation and uniting himself with it in humble adoration, and accepting the signs of the exalted assembly and taking on its colouring.

The explanation of this point lies in the fact that the meaning of purification is changing a bad characteristic for a good one. The quality of everything depends on its fineness. The immediate cause of that change will also be whatever is closest and most suited to the thing to be changed. Now there is nothing closer to the human soul than the supreme manifestation; and of all the qualities of Divinity, the one which accords with the qualities of the human soul is none other than to unite with that Supreme Being and adore it. Thus, whoever seeks the purification of the soul through pure unity, or through its preliminaries, has taken the wrong path. Hence the clear instructions given by the Law to turn our attention towards the Supreme Being.

At this point an extremely sacred truth emerges, which will require a moment's careful consideration. People through the ages have differed on one point, and the judgment concerning that difference is beset with perplexity.

Some people say that the fundamental purpose is total annihilation in the Divinity and complete withdrawal from the world of particularization—in short, the requirements of the hidden faculties. The Lawgiver has clearly explained that basic principle; he has invited those who have the capacity to approach that fundamental purpose, and brought detailed knowledge of it to their ears. The close attention shown to matters of life-style, and the establishment of bodily acts of devotion have been introduced into the Law because, in view of the fact that not everyone is able to fulfil the fundamental purpose, it does not follow that just because one cannot manage the whole thing, one has to give everything up. The former mode has the force of an obligatory ordinance, since it is what was originally intended; while the latter is more of a dispensation, being based as it is on man's faithlessness.

There are others who say that anything other than the course laid down by the outward form of the Law is undesirable, and that to affirm such a course is in fact contrary to the Law. Thus, to mention the knowledge of the hidden faculties is some kind of heresy.

Our own view on this is that the desired objective with regard to the human species is no more nor less than the purification of the bodily members and organs through actions, and the purification of the manifest faculties by means of states and stages. The human race has come into being in such a manner that its happiness lies in turning its attention towards the supreme manifestation and the exalted assembly; while its wretchedness lies in deviating from these.

Human beings had fallen into such a condition that most of them would have been punished in the intermediate world[3] and in the world to come. Mere thought alone would not have been enough to deliver them from such dire straits. Merciful God—exalted be his glory!—came to their assistance and established a way out for them. He sent them an interpreter of the language of the invisible world—the Holy Prophet, who was a man of their own kind. This was done in order that God's favour towards them might be complete, and that the supreme power which had required their creation in the first place might come to their aid a second time.

Thus, the very condition of mankind itself cried out for nothing more nor less than the imposition by the Source of Bounty of the Law and the purification of the bodily members and manifest faculties. Other than these influences, nothing else is required to ensure the needs of the species and the penetration of specific properties to the individual level. What the Law and the purification of the manifest faculties require is a carrier medium to root them firmly in the specific form. This implies that indi-

[3] Between death and resurrection.

viduals are required, but individuality does not really come into it. As for the annihilation of spiritual existence, the permanency of the Divinity, and the obliteration of the manifest faculties under the influence of the hidden faculties: none of these is necessary as far as the species is concerned. Sometimes, however, these things are required in the case of certain special individuals who have been created with extremely exalted and subtle capacities; hence a natural inclination is lodged in them towards these stages of attainment, and they are inspired with an ardent longing for them. Because of their individual qualities they are called in that direction, and eagerly they hurry there.

It is part of the wisdom of omniscient God to perfect any person who is perfectible, and to make the reality and the properties of that perfection easy for him to understand, and to enable him to reach his desired goal. 'Of the bounties of thy Lord we bestow freely on all—these as well as those: the bounties of thy Lord are not restricted.'[4]

However this process is most emphatically not one of the universal divine decrees, nor does it come under the heading of a major impulse issuing from the specific form. It is rather a particular law relating to certain individuals—a minor impulse issuing from a particular selfhood. The words of the Lawgiver never convey such an idea either explicitly or implicitly.

To be true, there are people who when they hear certain words of the Lawgiver are reminded of these matters, just as when someone hears the story of Laila and Majnun, he may evoke his own past adventures. However, it is our understanding that the intention of the Lawgiver is to conceal those secrets and keep silence about them, so that whoever is capable will understand, and whoever is not capable will remain in his natural way of thinking and will thus be saved from falling into multiple error and confusion, which is an incurable disease. The writings of Sufis may well be an amazingly effective alchemy for the specially gifted, but for the masses they can be a deadly

[4] Qur'an 17.20.

poison. God's blessing on whoever hides them from the eyes of the unworthy!

However, now that 'the cup has fallen from the roof', and it has become impossible nowadays to conceal these things any longer, a divine impulse has stimulated an inclination in my mind to specify the correct meaning of these things, and to explain this knowledge with a clarity and plainness that few have previously achieved. And I should now like to affirm that this knowledge is not what is meant by the Law, and that to ascribe such a meaning to the words of the Lawgiver is not correct—except by way of subjective association. 'And that is the decree of the Mighty, the Knowing.' However hard these words may seem to the mystics of today, I have been given a task to perform, and it is on that account that I say this. I am not concerned with what this or that person may think.

Concerning the knowledge relating to these hidden faculties, it should be remembered that because they are so extremely obscure, a large number of mistakes have been made, with the result that seekers have been considerably confused at every turn. They struggled in vain to understand, and ended up talking nonsense. It would therefore seem appropriate to turn our attention next to the question of what has caused so many mistakes. After that, if time permits, we should also consider the remedy for some of these errors. We should not, however, abandon anything that is utterly fundamental. May God help you and show you the realities of things as they really are!

The external senses of hearing and seeing, etc., have their own particular perceptions, such as colours, shapes, sizes and sounds. If we try to use these external senses to perceive anything other than their own objects of perception, they will not understand them at all. On the contrary: as far as the senses are concerned, anything else simply does not exist. For example if we used vision to try to perceive hunger, anger or shame, it would take these things to be totally non-existent, and would be able to gather nothing whatsoever about them. Indeed it might even establish a proof for their non-existence, and say that anything existing must be red or green, etc.; and since these things are not of that kind, they cannot exist. Thus by thinking in terms of opposites and the removal of opposites it would become further and further removed from the realm of really existing things. However, intelligent people are well aware that this is an error which results from judging the invisible on the basis of the visible, and mingling familiar properties with unfamiliar ones.

In the same way, the inner senses, such as imagination, fantasy and volition, also have their own perceptions. Now if these faculties are used for perceptions other than these, they will merely become bewildered, and their own properties will be disturbed. Perhaps they might fashion a proof from the ground-rules they have learnt, and from it establish the non-existence of those other things. For example, they might say that if the abstract exists, but does not exist in three-dimensional space, then logically this amounts to a juxtaposition of opposites: since to exist and yet not exist in space is self-contradictory. Intelligent people realize, however, that this is an error, and that once again the cause of it lies in judging the invisible on the basis of the visible, and mixing the familiar order with the unfamiliar.

Similarly the intellect, which is the tongue of the sublime spirit, has a certain range of perceptions within which it may freely move and act. But once the intellect moves beyond the range of what it can perceive, then it becomes perplexed and its properties are disturbed. Then it may perhaps establish a way to demonstrate the non-existence of these things, and from the familiar sciences which it has learnt, it may fashion a proof on which it can rely.

Men of intellect habitually dispute amongst themselves over subjects such as these; and it even happens that a single intellectual will contradict himself on two separate occasions. Meanwhile the knotty problem remains, and no progress is made. The actual cause of the dispute lies beyond the scope of the intellect, and is reckoned, by way of analogy and resemblance, to be one of the concepts. Such a person then proceeds to think that whatever transcends the intellect must be one of the concepts, and so includes it in this category; but because the resemblance is so tenuous, he is unable to understand clearly, and he lumps all the various properties together, simply judging them all to be beyond the scope of the intellect.

Then on another occasion our thinker, or perhaps some other intelligent person, fails to perceive some of the necessary consequences of that concept. So his former conviction is undermined; and he either remains bewildered or else repudiates the conviction. Or it may be that at some other time he himself, or some other intellectual, assumes that whatever lies beyond the scope of the intellect must belong to another type of concept altogether, and thus includes it in that other category. Thus a contradiction plainly emerges between these two trains of thought. The fact of the matter is that it does not belong to any conceptual category whatsoever. The analogies which have been drawn are fallacious, or else are simply some poetical fancy remembered from somewhere or other. It is this that lies at the root of all their disputations; and those who have failed to grasp this point are as a consequence forever locked in conflict, 'one with a sickle, one with a pick'.

Those followers of the philosophers, who entertain doctrines opposed to those of the Prophets, are in my opinion so many dogs. No, worse than dogs: after all, a dog does not smell old bones; while those vile wretches smell and lick bones that are two thousand years old. The cause of their error lies precisely in the defects of the intellect; and yet '...they rejoice in what knowledge they possess'. The intellect is indeed a great and impenetrable veil.

Let us look at the matter more closely. The intellect is the tongue of the spirit and its jurisdiction extends to whatever is of a like subtlety with the spirit. How true that saying is, that an entity cannot perceive other than itself or what is like itself. The spirit is neither a pure abstraction, nor is it something which can serve as a receptacle for things existing in the external world. Rather it is particularized in the external world and is a particular bubble in the midst of the external ocean. It lies within the scope of the intellect to comprehend the properties of the external world and the particular entities it comprises, and also the properties of the combination comprising the spatial and the abstract. For example, when the intellect sees individual humans, horses or donkeys, it can understand the characteristics which are shared by the individuals of each species. From here it can progress further and recognize and determine the specific form of each species. What induces it to arrive at this understanding is, on the one hand, the differences among existing things as to colour, shape, size, sound, etc., and, on the other hand, their underlying unity. But at the very point where multiplicity should be cast aside and the unity within unity should be perceived, the intellect is crippled and handicapped.

For example, it is the work of the intellect to fashion forms from tangible things, the essence of which is not in the external world at all, but is rather the source from which the forms derive. Then by a process of breaking-down and recombining, it brings a variety of distinct qualities to light. When it observes the sky it fashions the concept 'above', when it looks at the earth it derives the concept 'below', and when it sees a boy with his father it derives the attribute 'son'.

The intellect observes individual human beings, and from this it forms the concept of a universal human form. After closely scrutinizing individual specimens of man, horse, donkey, camel, cattle and sheep, it reduces these to an animal form. Then close scrutiny of individual animals and plants leads to the conceptual form of organic life. Each one of these concepts has an original source from which it has been abstracted. But neither the various sources nor the different specific forms actually appear to the intellect, nor are they portrayed to it in any way. All it sees are accidental configurations and nothing else. However, there does exist a path from contingent accidents back to their essential substance. Instinctively, the source extricates itself from the accidental and approaches the essential. In such matters of abstraction, many an absurdity becomes possible, and many an impossibility assumes the garb of existence. From this there proceeds a whole sequence of things which are considered to be permissible concerning the notion of abstraction; and the sequence only ceases when abstraction itself ceases.

Among such matters is the question of the absolutely non-existent and the absolutely unknown, both of which notions are firmly established in the intellect and form the basis for verifying many genuine precepts. In point of fact, however, there are discrepancies and incompatibilities in the very essence of this concept as well as in the precepts adduced from it. If there is such a thing as absolute non-existence, then how can it become present in the mind? If it is present in the mind, then how can it be called absolute non-existence? In fact the intellect has fashioned a mental picture and made it stand in for non-existence as a substitute. In this case the intellect is like someone with a squint who sees one thing as two, but realizes that he does so, and thus does not mistake the nature of the outside world. Or it is like someone who has placed a piece of green glass over his eye, and thus sees the whole world as green, even though he knows all the while that the world is not green. In the same way, the intellect is aware of the error of the intellect, and is thus not deflected from the path.

In short, we may describe the intellect as a faculty in which primary and secondary concepts are represented. It is here that the analytical teachings and proofs of the Law belong. The intellect can comprehend certain realities directly, and certain others only behind a veil, as it were. However close it may come to subtlety, it is connected and its attention is directed to the faculties of comprehension and thought, which have been located in the centre of the brain. The intellect is the tongue of the sublime spirit and is one of its faculties. Whatever involves discrimination and investigation is entrusted to it.

Its inward aspect is the secret faculty. At the time of unification with the supreme manifestation or the exalted assembly, the intellect perceives that inward aspect, but its perception is mixed and confused. When it comes down a little from this state, that same perception becomes the hearing and vision of the spirit.

If anyone uses the word intellect instead of the word 'taste', his speech does not accord with conventional language, but there is no harm in that. According to us the word taste is used to describe perception in which there is no abstraction of concepts and no room for the analytical teachings and proofs of the Law. Such a perception is in fact 'the presence of a thing by itself, for itself, in itself and of itself'. It comes into contact with whatever forms the surface of these various bubbles and attaches itself externally to the first part which emerges from them. Thus when the visible qualities have been observed, and a search is made for the invisible qualities, none of these are actually found to be present. But the secret faculty, which is given over to glorification, is in evidence in an imitative role; and these qualities are taken to refer to such imitation. The intellect understands a separate meaning for each quality, and recognizes separate consequences for each meaning. When some of these consequences are found to be incompatible with others, the intellect becomes perplexed and loses its grasp. In fact the above has been more of an analysis of the error made by the intellect, and only a brief summary of the faculty of taste. The contradiction mentioned above has its root in contradictions in sense perception, and it is to these in fact that this analysis should return. It is like our man with a squint, who sees one thing as two.

One should not imagine that the analytical teachings and proofs of the Law can rescue the intellect from this error. Far from it. Such pronouncements and demonstrations are simply a classification and presentation of the things that are stored up by the intellect in order that from this material God may create a creation which might explain the issue. It is just the same as when God creates the form of a tree or a mineral from water, air and earth: this creation is simply lodged in its own material; it is no more subtle or sublime than that. It is idle to look for meat in a plate of sweets.

When this proposition has been absorbed, it should be realized that the greatest mistake which people make in this area is to assert that 'All is God'. When subsequently they find such a colossal difference between the consequences to be inferred from total subservience on the one hand and absolute dominion on the other, they become utterly confused. The rectification of this error is based on two premises: first, that there is a misunderstanding concerning the relationship that exists between these various bubbles and the external world; and, second, that there is a misunderstanding concerning the relationship existing between the external world and the Pure Essence.

Regarding the first premise it should be understood that the world of appearance is a relationship between manifesting form and manifest phenomenon, and this relationship is of a different order from other relationships. Form and phenomenon are not identical in every respect, any more than the human species is identical with individual humans. If the species were identical with one particular individual in every respect, then it would follow that one individual would likewise be completely interchangeable with another. On the other hand, if the species were different from the individual in all respects, then it would be impossible to say: 'This is a man', or even: 'This is a stone'.

Similarly, we have seen that the species man and horse may be linked together in the collective term animal; animal and plant collectively come under the heading organism; organism and chemical compound both belong to the category physical body; concrete body and abstract idea are both subsumed in the term essence, while essence and accident go to make up the relationship termed universal soul. From our verification of the reality of one thing in relation to another, it is apparent that there are as many indications of similarity as there are of difference; and hence there is scope for both modes of approach.

When we investigate and thoroughly analyse the relationship which exists between the characteristics of the universe and those of the universal soul, and ascend from height to height, we find that this relationship is only one of appearance. The perplexity which the intellect experiences with regard to these disparate characteristics derives from its own failure to understand, and from the clash of self-evident premisses, which we have already noted.

It may be objected that, if all of this is manifested in one thing, then where did all the separate properties come from? And if all the sources are independent, then how can they all be merged into one source? This amounts to contradicting a self-evident premiss. The answer to this is that in the case of individuals in relation to their species we have accepted precisely this relationship. If the question is raised whether or not the source of plurality is originally one, we may reply that in the first case that source cannot be one, and in the second case there is nowhere from which it could have arisen. Besides, this would be a contradiction of a self-evident premiss. In fact the single source we are discussing here is not synonymous with that one which is possessed of real oneness.

The emanation from the Holy Unity and the descent to the second stage is enough to produce all this plurality. Certain deficient intellects occasionally take this to be the same thing in all respects; but when some of the logical consequences of such an identity are found to be lacking, then that conviction is demolished. At other times they may take it to be totally different in every respect; but when certain logical consequences of that non-identity are not to be found, they become confused. However, sound intellects are well aware that it is a relationship which is neither totally identical nor totally different.

Whatever may be the peculiarities which have arisen in individual cases, the field of the universal soul is itself free from all such defects—in just the same way as the human species remains untarnished by such defects as darkness of skin, shortness of stature or a stammer; even though this particular short, dark stutterer is undeniably a human being. Similarly it is impossible to attribute the species, the universal or the absolute, to a particular individual, no matter how much the absolute may be restricted.

If the reality of the universal soul is unconditionally accepted, in such a way that no other viewpoint except the reality of the universal soul is contemplated, either negatively or positively, then the properties of absoluteness and restriction may both be accommodated without doing violence to the purity of that reality. There remain two points to be considered.

First, there are many other species besides the human species; thus there are many other specific characteristics besides those of the human species. As a result of weighing up the variations which occur, the intellect becomes convinced of the existence of the various species and can tell each one from the next. However, there is nothing perceptible to sense or reason alongside the universal soul, so that in keeping with the dictum: 'Things are known by their opposites', men's minds might act freely within it and might be able to tell it apart from other things. For all of time it is by itself and in itself: never has it turned towards itself with renewed attention; in no circumstances has it ever sought to reinvestigate itself. And yet for all that, it is subtlety within subtlety, simplicity within simplicity, '... exempt from any taint of attachment'.

Even if the intellect were to try, it could never attain to

this grace: the only result would be bewilderment. However, those who are endowed with the faculty of taste can indeed perceive this by way of 'the presence of a thing for itself, with itself, and in itself'. As a result their intellect receives a hint of that condition. Such people are thus like the man who has a squint and yet is aware of the fact: somehow he manages to find out the true situation and make himself familiar with the unfamiliar.

> I have no way of knowing
> the caravan my love is in;
> but the tinkling of my camel's bell
> can be heard from afar.

The second point is this: the philosophers have failed to establish the true common factor between the essential substance and the contingent accident, and have thus not recognized the universal soul as the highest genus. The reason for this is the total annihilation which supervenes in the presence of the universal soul. According to their intellect, the testimony of someone concerning that which is witnessed for and by itself, and which cannot be known to the intellect, is simply not to be credited.

We ourselves are well aware that one reality can appear in two different forms. Sometimes it appears in its self-subsistent mode, and is known as the essential substance; at other times it subsists by virtue of something else, in which case it is called the accident:

> Sometimes descending in Laila's guise,
> sometimes arising in the shape of Majnun.

One of the fascinating things about this subject is that in the world of ideas accidents become essential substance; and, conversely, essential substances become accidents in the domain of imagination, with the mental picture accurately matching external existence.

Concerning the second premiss, mentioned above, there is indeed a relationship between the Creator and the created, the like of which is not to be found in the visible world, so that creation could be actualized in matter and hence produce differentiation and independence. It is, however, not a question of a length of time, in which what precedes may be separated and distinguished from what succeeds. It has no permanence other than its Origin, and it has no reality other than in, with and through this. On every side it is encompassed and embraced by the Creator. Here the intellect is bewildered and confused. It has adopted abstract concepts, which it has fashioned into evidence of the relationship between the Creator and the created, it has represented to itself all manner of contrived edifices, and shot every bolt it had in its quiver. God forbid! The great gulf between Creator and created is a figment of the imagination: between the two there is not even space for so much as one hair to pass. Where would there be room for such absurd suppositions? But: 'Half a hair is a great deal—if it happens to be in your eye.'

The intellect made use of all the terms which it had established to describe effects and phenomena in the visible world. Sometimes it spoke in terms of something created or made; sometimes it recalled an adjective or a noun; on other occasions it spoke in terms of ascent and descent. For each of these it found a proof of sorts by way of analogy; but it was never able to pin-point their reality in every detail. And so it recoiled in confusion:

> I repented my words:
> for words had no meaning,
> and meaning no words.

What has been ascertained about the question of creativity is that its existence is known but its nature is unknown. It is not entirely a descent from above, nor is it an ascent into being from below. Thus the extreme difficulties which have arisen out of trying to establish each separate one of these realities in detail are not experienced here. However, when certain people of intuition looked deep within themselves the universal soul appeared to them. They gave it the name of 'being', and discerned in it such subtlety and simplicity, far transcending the scope of rational thought, that they supposed it to be precisely the self-existent Divine Being. Subsequently, whenever any simple or subtle thing reached them, they made it accord with that Being, and were content to remain forever with this degree of knowledge. They did not realize: 'How far still the climb to the carefree bed of ease.'

If you wish to understand this teaching more clearly then it is essential that you should grasp this cardinal point. The cause of this error lies in false information concerning the universal soul, and the fact that these people contented themselves with what was merely one of its aspects and did not encompass all its dimensions. Had they understood the universal soul in depth, they would never have called it the Origin of Origins.

There are others who have passed beyond the universal soul and understood the Pure Essence as the First of the First, and the universal soul as the first emanation and unfolding of being into the manifold forms of existence. However they mixed all of this together, gave it one name and lumped it all together under one heading. They mixed up some realities with others and classified the most subtle of them as the inward aspects of the others. It is an old habit of the Sufis to give several things the same name; so there is nothing new about this. 'It isn't the first bottle ever to be broken.' We have already alluded to this in the section dealing with the spirit and the secret faculty.

On account of this laxity of interpretation, certain impatient individuals have even opposed this type of investigation, saying that all of this is one and the same Being, who appears different owing to differences in standpoint. From the standpoint of its connection with the various realities it is the self-unfolding Being, while from the perspective of its own purity it is the Pure Essence. The cause of this confusion lies in the total failure to discriminate between the relationship which the various realities have with the universal soul and the relationship which the universal soul has with the Origin of Origins.

There were certain people whose intuition was linked with the supreme manifestation, others who inductively established the stable attributes of necessity, and yet others who through their superficial observance of the Law had placed their faith in counterfeit, imitative qualities. When these various properties were not found in the universal soul, nor were they verified in the things which the gnostics brought back from the Pure Essence, then these various types of people protested and denied both of the aforementioned relationships.

What we have managed to ascertain concerning the Pure Essence is that, from the standpoint of its relationship with the supreme manifestation and its special connections with the reflections and lights which radiate from the latter, it does indeed possess many properties; however, intuition, inductive proof and the superficial observance of the Law have no way to pass beyond this field and have no idea whatsoever about what lies outside it. God knows best the realities of things.

Chapter Seven

THOUGHTS AND THEIR CAUSES

The science of the faculties is complemented by the knowledge of the various types of thought which occur to the mind. Thus in this area, too, there are a number of points which have to be understood.

Any thought which occurs within a man's mind partakes of one of the following three situations:

It takes place in the heart alone. Thoughts of this kind are called 'states' and 'moments': such emotions as fear, hope, depression, elation, love, regret, grief, etc.

Alternatively it may take place in the intellect alone, sometimes in the form of a disclosure of future events, sometimes as a premonition.

The third situation arises when it is located in both the heart and the intellect. The intellect imagines and formulates a certain thing, while the heart provides the necessary resolution. Such thoughts are known as impulses.

It is a matter of the utmost importance to be able to distinguish genuine thoughts from false ones, if there are to be no defects in the actions arising from such thoughts. This is of course impossible without a knowledge of what it is that causes thoughts; hence it is essential to reiterate the various causes of thoughts.

Sometimes the occurrence of a thought is the result of the way in which the intellect, heart and self are constituted—just as, for example, hunger, thirst, lust or coldness give rise to a particular impulse. It may be that love for someone calls for a meeting; or perhaps the black humour spreads dark temptations which lead to like actions; or else the yellow humour occasions bilious fantasies leading to depression, hard-heartedness or garrulousness. Habit also serves as a cause for the behaviour of the self.

The intellect has been given the power of perception, while the power of decision and intention is located in the heart; and it is in accordance with this disposition that they exercise control. However, all of this produces a confused jumble of thoughts, which the seeker is at pains to avoid; indeed he suppresses and eradicates anything which might hinder the fruitful use of his time.

Occasionally a thought arises in the mind of such a person which is the result of demonic control. By demons we mean malignant souls which infiltrate the finer elements; their basic motive is to create melancholy, indecision, greed and the breakdown of good order, whether in the spiritual, domestic, social or national domain. Order is in general to be preferred, whatever that order may be: it is a prerequisite of the mercy of God; and to undermine that order will inevitably entail his anger. Such behaviour is to be attributed to demons.

When as a result either of heavenly or acquired causes, a man becomes receptive to the influx of such impulses and thoughts, then hordes of demons, in keeping with their nature, turn their attention towards him and pour into his heart the impulses typical of themselves. Certain impure souls also join in with the demons and actively participate in their work. The impulses of demons always create melancholy, indecision and hardness of heart, in addition to diverting the individual from acts of kindness. Their promptings are merely calculated to produce base actions and the breakdown of good order. Nothing that percolates into the mind from these impure, malignant souls is free from fear and horror, and all of it is sheer deception. The seeker is lucky if he has the knowledge to repulse and drive out such thoughts and take refuge with God from them.

Sometimes the descent of thoughts is from the world of ideas, either with or without the agency of the angels appointed to that domain. The term 'world of ideas' is used to mean a coupling together of the aspirations and secrets both of the souls of the heavens and of the angels of the exalted assembly, seen collectively in a unified perspective. An analogy of the situation might be torches and candles of different kinds, varying in both size and brightness, which have been lit in a house, and from the totality of which a light is derived which in essence and quality is unified. In the same way the aspirations and secrets of this assemblage are gathered in the presence of the supreme manifestation, and the requirements of these aspirations are displayed without each thing being specifically referred back to its origin. When this form appeared to people of intuition, and it went beyond their powers of expression to describe the essential reality of the situation, they designated a label for it, namely the world of ideas.

The angels who serve the world of ideas are the serene souls who penetrate a body composed of the subtle elements in a completely balanced state. This occurs when there is an auspicious conjunction of the stars and the sublime world has an affinity for Pure Goodness. Hence these souls are all repose within repose, happiness within happiness, and for the world of ideas they are the embodiment of submission and veneration.

Angels come into being at different times and consequently become attached to different spheres. In accordance with its original nature, each angel has the capacity to receive inspiration in a particular matter. All the various impulses which pour down from the world of ideas into the hearts of angels belong to one of two types.

The first type occurs when there is a particular conjunction of the stars, as a result of which a universal event is represented and established as an ideal with an existence of its own in the presence of the supreme manifestation. In such a case people say, 'God wrote such and such, or decided such and such'. This universal event then descends at the proper time and place. The angels in the service of that descending event strive hard on its behalf, and if they intuitively recognize anyone who is by nature equal to that event, they bring him closer to it by means alternately of contraction and expansion. Thus from their own aspirations are effected the necessary transmission and inspiration, and the desired object is achieved.

The second type of impulse occurs in the following way. Every essential substance and every accidental manifestation possesses a specific requirement; and human souls have their own particular destiny. Thus the universal soul does not come down itself into the particular soul, but rather adapts itself to the form of the world obtaining on that particular day. The requirement of the particular soul, which will inevitably be modelled on the actual form of the world, is called destiny; and each man will fare according to his own particular destiny.

When these forces come into close proximity with one another, and the special characteristics of things become differentiated, then a decree is issued and universal nature becomes organized into particulars. This is analogous to the situation when water is poured on to uneven ground which is strewn with sticks and straws and stones and clods of earth: when the water collides with these various obstacles, it is in the nature of water to percolate through. The same thing occurs with the collision of forces: a decree pours down from universal nature, and hosts of angels adapted to that inspiration hasten to be present in the battlefield and control the situation by means of inspiration, transmission, contraction and expansion, until that decree is made manifest and the imagined form comes into existence.

The action of the angels in this case is comparable to the action of nature working in a body when a disease reaches its crisis. Or it is like the metamorphosis of insects according to the requirements of their natures, or the way that moths mob round a lamp. It is according to such a pattern that impulses descend into the hearts of mankind.

Sometimes the angels contrive a stratagem to save someone from destruction. Sometimes they make a person aware of the real situation by means of dreams or voices. At other times they may use someone else, or even an animal, as a means to convey some information to the individual or to do something for him.

Most of such thoughts percolate through via the energies of the world of ideas. The angels make no distinction between good and bad in their work of transmission and inspiration. In addition to the many angels of humanity, there is also a band of pure souls who do the work of angels and are thus counted among their number.

The science of talisman, the science of letters, and the science of the names of God, all derive from a knowledge of this system or from a branch of it. And God knows best.

Be that as it may, the impulses and thoughts which are numbered among the stages of perfection come under one of three headings.

The first category is when a thought descends from the major selfhood into the minor selfhood. The reason for this descent is an inherent part of the system, in that the universal expediency required the establishment of some benefit or other in the world. Now the establishment of a benefit without the mediation of one particular human being would not be possible. To be more precise, when the form of the world changes and the condition of its basic components also changes, then it follows of necessity that the supreme manifestation should also move from one state to another. This is the meaning implied in the words 'Every day He is in a new state.'[1]

The exalted assembly takes on this same colouring. There can be no affinity with Pure Goodness except by immersion in this influence. Hence it is essential in this case that human souls should be tinged with the colouring of this holy presence, and that it should permeate them through and through.

This is analogous to the situation when water comes into contact with some earth: inevitably some of the water will soak through the soil, and by virtue of the porosity of the earth will seep through to the other side of the intervening mass. In this case, however, the 'pores' belong to the souls of the exalted assembly and those of

[1] Qur'an 55.29.

perfected individuals. It is they alone who have pores and channels connecting them with the major selfhood and the supreme manifestation, which last is the heart, as it were, of the major selfhood. Thus it is that this impulse, passing via universal nature, reaches these perfected souls and from there connects up with all other souls.

The aspirations of the exalted assembly are like enclosed waters: as long as they are not stirred up, they will not stir up by themselves. Or, again, they are like a spring: as long as no one scoops up a handful of water from it, it will not reach the thirsting mouth. The difference between the aspirations of the exalted assembly as a whole and those of a single individual from its midst is analogous to the difference which is to be seen between the prior knowledge that an astronomer possesses about eclipses in general and the knowledge which people gain about one particular eclipse when they actually see it taking place. So long as this general aspiration does not become a particular one, the universal expediency will not descend in the form of a particular expedient act, and the precipitation from that majestic presence will not be able to flow continuously, linking pore to pore.

Such an impulse then selects one of those perfected souls. First of all it produces an expansion in his pure intellect, which is thus enabled to mingle and associate with the supreme manifestation. Then that impulse descends into his pure intellect, in the way that a signet ring stamps its impression in wax. Subsequently both the secret faculty and the spirit become amenable to its will. The pattern of that impulse is transferred from the exalted assembly, just like the imprint of the ring on the wax; from there it descends further to the intellect and the heart, thus colouring the premonitions of the mind and the states of the heart. This impulse becomes an authoritative pronouncement, and can appear in new forms according to the requirements of the circumstances. After that, the impulse descends further to the level of the physical body, and induces the people to act in accordance with that truth.

Thus a new religion, or doctrine, or line of succession is organized. God then pours down a fresh enhancement into the knowledge of the perfect man, and inspires his religion and his doctrine, so that they may continue through the ages, uneffaced. Successive reformers then revive that religion, until eventually the complexion of the supreme manifestation changes, and this new aspect appears within the heart of another perfected man. Most probably the supreme manifestation will appear to him to be tinged with the colour of that new impulse. Thus whatever news he gives of the supreme manifestation will contain a hint of that new colouring.

There is one point here which should be carefully noted: the best interpreter of the truth is the one whose intellect keeps silent concerning the premonitions and thoughts which arise spontaneously within his mind by virtue of its own innate disposition. Apart from the impulse which we have described above, nothing stirs his intellect or prompts him to any original utterance. The most perfect exemplification of this is to be found in Muhammad, the Seal of the Prophets. Jesus Christ proclaimed the unification of the pure intellect with the supreme manifestation, thereby creating a mighty stir. The Holy Prophet, however, did not speak of this matter either overtly or covertly. Whatever he said was said calmly and with complete sobriety of mind.

We now come to the second category of thoughts and impulses. The training of human souls has its equivalent in the world of ideas, and this is the concern of the universal impulse. However it is essential that a particular impulse should be joined with it. Thus this impulse percolates down into the hearts of upright people who are continuously devoted to the world of ideas and to the angels who are the bearers of this secret. The desire to carry out this work arises in a great number of people, and through them it is brought to completion. Spiritual leaders, reformers of religion, even the guide who is the very axis of the earth, all drink their fill at this fountain.

It may even be that perfected individuals likewise receive this secret from the presence of the world of ideas and exert themselves accordingly, but in such a case they would be working below their true capacity. Or it may be that some of those matters which we have already discussed pour down on the angels of humanity; in which case it is for them to make the appropriate effort.

Sometimes it happens that inspiration is directed towards a certain person, but that the import of that inspiration is conveyed via the speech of someone else, who may or may not know the underlying situation and the intention behind what he says. In such a case the latter would appear to the former to be one of the angels. Or it might even be that he is brought to an understanding of that inspiration through the cooing of a dove, the chirping of a sparrow, or the sound made by some object or other.

The third and final category is this: the luminous angels appointed to watch over the exercises of praise and submission circle round whoever performs them and some of their splendour falls upon his intellect and his heart. If the heart is uppermost then the quality of the resultant state is one of intimacy and tranquillity. But if the intellect is predominant, the blessing takes the form of premonitions, or else the resolve of his heart becomes linked with the intention to perform good actions; such an intention is consistent with the understanding of the angels, and is therefore known as 'angelic thought'.

Sometimes this same state or thought is represented to the perception of the seeker in sleep. In the first case that sleep becomes a dream of splendour and bliss and everything connected with intimacy and tranquillity. In the second case it takes the form of an admonition, the substance of which is the command either to perform a certain act or to desist from doing an evil one. This is in fact a revelation of the mind which has appeared in the individual's intellect and created there the form of an impulse.

Here this treatise entitled *The Sacred Knowledge of the*

Higher Functions of the Mind comes to an end. It is to God that all praise is due, first and last, outwardly and inwardly. May God shower his blessings and benedictions upon our Lord Muhammad and his family and descendants.